15/6/24

SAS

The Illustrated History

SAS

WHO DARES WINS

The Illustrated History

BARRY DAVIES, BEM

DEDICATION

The Special Air Service

Although this is not an official history of the Special Air Service, it portrays the regiment with a high degree of accuracy. I should know; I served with the regiment for eighteen years. Having established myself as a writer, with a great deal of my work based around my experiences in the SAS, at a time when the regiment is anxious to shun unsolicited publicity, I have decided that this book will be my last on the SAS. I hope that this will help to return some measure of normality to the proliferation of works being written about the SAS. In light of this, I dedicate this book to the officers and men of 22 SAS, both past and present.

Acknowledgements

The author would like to thank all those ex-members of the SAS who provided pictures for this book. They have all asked not to be named, and specified that where the soldiers in shot are still serving, their faces should be blanked. The publisher's decision was to blank every face to avoid any chance of an individual being put in any danger. Secondly, and with the knowledge that the Special Air Service Regiment has suffered by the recent release of SAS books, I hope that they find *SAS - The Illustrated History*, more in keeping with their current image. Until now Tony Geraghty has always produced, with the regiment's help, a wonderful and accurate history of the SAS. Unfortunately, his research material was not available to me, but having been a serving member of the SAS for   eighteen years, I do have access to a vast array of fascinating photographs which bring this book to life.

My thanks also go to the Photographic Department of the Imperial War Museum, Section Five studios of Stockport, Photo Press and Frank Spooner.

ISBN 1 85227 681 9

First published in Great Britain in 1996 by
Virgin Books
an imprint of Virgin Publishing Ltd
332 Ladbroke Grove
London W10 5AH

A catalogue record for this book is available from the British Library.

ISBN 1 85227 696 7

Designed by Design 23, London
Printed in Italy
Colour separations by Pendry Litho, Hove, England

Disclaimer.

Before I undertook this project, I took serious legal advice regarding the reproduction of the photographs used in this book. I have complied with the law, in so much as I hold many of the original negatives, slides, or Polaroids. Where I do not have the original negative, slide or Polaroid, then I have the owner's consent in writing for the rights connected with publication of the photographs. Additionally, some of the photographic rights have been purchased from various sources in the belief that the vendor holds such rights. Where there has been any doubt as to ownership, every reasonable effort has been made to locate the true owner of the each picture.

CONTENTS

CHAPTER ONE
THE EARLY YEARS 8

CHAPTER TWO
SELECTION AND TRAINING 28

CHAPTER THREE
COMBAT SURVIVAL 52

CHAPTER FOUR
TROOP TRAINING 66

CHAPTER FIVE
OMAN 82

CHAPTER SIX
NORTHERN IRELAND 106

CHAPTER SEVEN
ANTI-TERRORIST TEAM 122

CHAPTER EIGHT
COUNTER-REVOLUTIONARY WARFARE 154

CHAPTER NINE
THE FALKLANDS 172

CHAPTER TEN
THE GULF WAR 182

CHAPTER ELEVEN
SPECIALS AND SURPRISES 212

CHAPTER TWELVE
ROLL OF HONOUR 220

OPERATIONAL HISTORY 223

INTRODUCTION

Many years ago, while serving as a sergeant in the Special Air Service, and a keen photographer to boot, my Squadron Commander asked me to produce a photo album. Using the vast collection in my personal possession, and gathering many others that were freely offered, I set about the task. Most pictures were of the boys doing different things, and many were only posed shots of individuals, but just a few were rather unique. The album, which seemed like a good idea at the time, fell by the wayside as operations once more demanded our immediate attention. I kept the photographs together, dragging them with me from house to house, even from country to country, and unfortunately many were lost over the years. At last I have completed the album, and it stands as a tribute to the men, the training, the skills and the success of the SAS over the past 25 years. That said, although this is essentially a modern history, it would be amiss of me not to mention briefly the birth of the regiment, and its resurrection as 22 Special Air Service during the early 1950s.

They say a picture is worth a thousand words and, in the case of the *SAS Illustrated History*, there has never been a more accurate statement. This book contains scores of photographs, most of which have never been seen before. They cover the more recent history of the SAS and speak volumes about Britain's elite regiment, showing the tough training methods that members of the British Army must endure in order to wear the coveted winged dagger and giving a unique insight into SAS life, from training exercises to major operations all over the world.

The equipment and tactics used by the SAS have changed dramatically in recent years and the process of change is ongoing. The regiment keeps itself thoroughly up to date with modern technological developments and in many cases leads the way in producing new weapons and equipment. One thing, however, remains constant - the men. In truth, the personality of the SAS has changed little since the days of David Stirling back in WWII. What has changed is the enemy, and the threat he poses to our society. The men of the SAS have been asked to take on many and varied tasks over the years, facing each new challenge with the kind of determination and dedication that only such men can offer. To those who think that SAS soldiers are invincible, I would say that, in terms of skill and courage, they are indeed. Sadly, they are still men of flesh and blood, and many have died. They died protecting our country and our way of life. As one SAS soldier, long since dead, once stated, 'When they eat their breakfasts in the morning, and jump in their cars to go to work, do they ever think about us protecting the trade routes?' This soldier died in the Oman war, protecting British interests (oil) against the spread of communism.

As the war in Oman was being fought, a sinister new enemy was beginning to emerge - international terrorism. This began with several hijackings in the late 60s, most of which hit the headlines around the world, but nothing had prepared society for the 1972 Olympic Games massacre in Munich. This single act provoked a vast retaliation against terrorism. First it was Entebbe, then Mogadishu, and then came the Iranian Embassy siege in London. Above all else, this action by the SAS threw them on to centre stage, and they performed well. Not only that, but they did it in full view of a live television audience.

On a final note, many claim disparagingly that the SAS is nothing more than a bunch of highly trained killers. Highly trained, yes, and prepared to kill, certainly, but what are their real motivations? Why do you think they suffer the rigors of selection? Why does the government hone them, supply them with the very latest equipment, and dress them in black? They do so because when all else fails, and our country needs such men, they know that they can count on the Special Air Service. As for the men themselves, they are your sons, your brothers, husbands and fathers. They are good, just men, of whom we should be proud.

CHAPTER ONE

THE EARLY YEARS

Since its creation during World War II as a raiding force designed to cause havoc behind enemy lines in the deserts of North Africa, the SAS has dramatically widened its scope of operations, developing innovative new strategies and sophisticated, specialised equipment to help them tackle the most arduous tasks and the most deadly adversaries. There remain, however, striking similarities between the SAS soldier of 1941 and his modern-day counterpart in the Gulf War. The vehicles and equipment used in the Gulf may have been high-tech but the levels of personal fitness, courage, commitment and professionalism displayed by the SAS soldier of today bears testimony to the standards set in the desert more than 50 years ago.

The historical photographs seen here have been selected with care in order to show what the SAS was like in its early years. They represent the young SAS and demonstrate how the daring raids carried out behind the German lines, not just in North Africa but also in occupied France, Greece, Italy, Yugoslavia and throughout Europe, contributed so much to the Allied war effort. Destroying aircraft and disrupting lines of communication and supply became everyday tasks for the fledgling regiment. They established a ferocious reputation, but death was the only reward if they were captured.

The SAS grew into two regiments during the war and also had special French and Belgian detachments, but despite its success, was disbanded in 1945. By 1949, however, it was reborn in the form of the Malayan Scouts. These men fought for months in the hostile jungle, befriending the natives, stalking the communist terrorists and recreating the legend of the SAS.

In 1951, 22 SAS was formed and the newly expanded regiment went on to fight in Malaya, Oman, Aden and Borneo.

An SAS patrol in the North African desert during World War II. The guns are Vickers 'K' machine guns originally intended for use by aircraft but adapted to become the perfect weapon for hit-and-run raids. This raiding party had just returned after three months behind enemy lines. (IWM)

CHAPTER ONE

THE EARLY YEARS

Since its creation during World War II as a raiding force designed to cause havoc behind enemy lines in the deserts of North Africa, the SAS has dramatically widened its scope of operations, developing innovative new strategies and sophisticated, specialised equipment to help them tackle the most arduous tasks and the most deadly adversaries. There remain, however, striking similarities between the SAS soldier of 1941 and his modern-day counterpart in the Gulf War. The vehicles and equipment used in the Gulf may have been high-tech but the levels of personal fitness, courage, commitment and professionalism displayed by the SAS soldier of today bears testimony to the standards set in the desert more than 50 years ago.

The historical photographs seen here have been selected with care in order to show what the SAS was like in its early years. They represent the young SAS and demonstrate how the daring raids carried out behind the German lines, not just in North Africa but also in occupied France, Greece, Italy, Yugoslavia and throughout Europe, contributed so much to the Allied war effort. Destroying aircraft and disrupting lines of communication and supply became everyday tasks for the fledgling regiment. They established a ferocious reputation, but death was the only reward if they were captured.

The SAS grew into two regiments during the war and also had special French and Belgian detachments, but despite its success, was disbanded in 1945. By 1949, however, it was reborn in the form of the Malayan Scouts. These men fought for months in the hostile jungle, befriending the natives, stalking the communist terrorists and recreating the legend of the SAS.

In 1951, 22 SAS was formed and the newly expanded regiment went on to fight in Malaya, Oman, Aden and Borneo.

An SAS patrol in the North African desert during World War II. The guns are Vickers 'K' machine guns originally intended for use by aircraft but adapted to become the perfect weapon for hit-and-run raids. This raiding party had just returned after three months behind enemy lines. (IWM)

In 1940, David Stirling was a lieutenant with No 8 Commando in North Africa. In the belief that a small band of dedicated men could operate successfully behind the enemy lines, he went to great lengths to present his idea to the high command. Finally, he accosted General Ritchie, Deputy Chief of Staff, in his own office inside GHQ, having climbed a barbed wire fence and evaded all the sentries to get there. His idea and memorandum eventually reached the Commander in Chief of the Middle East, General Auchinleck, and the SAS was born. As the founder of the SAS, Stirling's main strength came from his ability to select and enlist those men who had both daring and vision. One such man was Paddy Mayne. (IWM)

Paddy Mayne was one of Stirling's first recruits on forming the SAS. The nickname 'Paddy' came with his Irish ancestry, and before the war he was well known for his accomplishments in the world of sport. In battle he possessed qualities of leadership which set him apart from most men; he was awarded four DSOs. His reputation was built on his personal bravery, which at times was characterised as reckless and wild. Indeed, when he was first recruited into the SAS, he was under arrest for striking a superior officer. Mayne survived the rigors of many SAS attacks deep behind enemy lines, only to be killed in a car crash in 1955. This photograph was taken on a visit to the War Office. (IWM)

Lieutenant Colonel Stirling talking to Lieutenant McDonald, the leader of the raiding party pictured previously. Although this photograph was taken in the desert, the heavy duffel coat worn by Stirling demonstrates how cold it can get, especially at night. (IWM)

An American Willy's jeep as used by the SAS. They were light, agile and robust, ideally suited to desert conditions because of their four-wheel drive. This one has a 0.5in Browning heavy machine gun on the front, with a single Vickers 'K' for the front passenger and a set of twin 'K's for the rear man. All the extra jerry cans contain either fuel or water. (IWM)

As early as 1942, the reputation of the SAS soldier was being born. This man, Cpl Sillito, walked over 100 miles back to friendly lines after a raid on the German railway system near Alamein. Cpl Sillito and a lieutenant, were tasked with taking care of any German guards. As they did so the lieutenant's machine gun jammed, and he died during the firefight. Sillito, pursued by the enemy, managed to escape. With no food or water, he covered the distance in just over two days. When he was finally found by members of his own unit, he was too weak to stand. (IWM)

Trucks of the Long Range Desert Group (LRDG) preparing for battle. The LRDG worked very closely with the SAS in the early years of the North African campaign. The similarity to the SAS fighting columns during the Gulf War is uncanny. (IWM)

His Royal Highness the Duke of Gloucester inspects troops who have been recommended for gallantry awards. Note the SAS wings on the chest of the soldiers. The same wings are used today, but they are now worn on the left arm. (IWM)

His Royal Highness inspects SAS troops as they strip and assemble German weapons. Knowing the enemy's weapons as well as your own is still a basic requirement for their modern-day counterparts. (IWM)

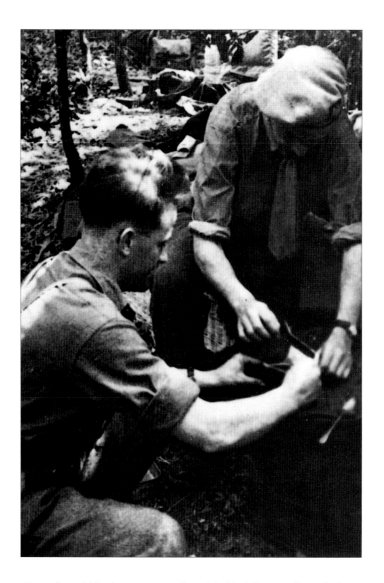

Men of 1st SAS who were parachuted behind German lines during Operation Bullbasket in June 1944. This picture of Lt H. Storres and Lt P.H.P. Weaver in a clandestine open-air camp was taken near Chateauroux. The purpose of Operation Bullbasket was to support the Normandy landings. (IWM)

Opposite top: Another picture from Operation Bullbasket. The man seated at the front is Johnie Holmes. All except Holmes were captured by the Germans on the 3rd July 1944 and executed four days later. Note the camouflage net concealing the jeep. (IWM)

Opposite bottom: French soil again, in the forest near Le Forêt de Verrieres. Standing is Capt J.E. Tonkin, sitting on the right is Lt H. Morris. The four others were captured by the Germans and executed on the 7th July 1944. (IWM)

During the war in Africa, the SBS (Special Boat Section, later to become Special Boat Service) established itself as part of 1st SAS. One of the greatest heroes of the SBS was the Danish Lieutenant Anders Lassen. Operating from bases in Turkey, the SBS raided German-held islands all round the Aegean and the Adriatic with Lassen always in the thick of the action. It was on the mainland in Italy, however, that a gross act of treachery brought about Lassen's demise. By this time promoted to Major, Lassen was leading a diversionary force during the attack on Lake Commachio, advancing along a road heavily defended by machine-gun nests and pill-boxes. The patrol came under vicious fire; one was wounded and the rest took cover in the lake. Lassen, however, pressed on with the attack. He destroyed the machine-gun nests and the first pill-box with grenades then moved forward armed with a pistol and grenades to knock out three more pill-boxes. The fifth pill-box hung out a white flag but when Lassen approached to accept their surrender, they opened fire and he was shot at close range. Lassen was only the second foreigner, the first also being a Dane, to win the Victoria Cross, awarded for his actions at Lake Commachio. He was 25 years old.

The birth of the modern-day 22 SAS came about during the communist troubles in Malaya between 1950 – 1959. Trouble had been brewing in Malaya for a couple of years and Lieutenant Colonel Mike Calvert, who was serving in Hong Kong at the time, was instructed to evaluate the communist influence. Calvert, a tough soldier who had commanded an SAS Brigade during the last war, innovated the idea of the Malayan Scouts (SAS). He instigated many of the basic tactics that exist today, the most famous being the four-man patrol. They performed and operated under very hostile conditions, completing arduous tasks deep within enemy territory. The Malayan Scouts formally became known as 22 SAS in 1951, whereupon Calvert instructed Major John Woodhouse to return to England and set up a specialised selection course. Calvert *(inset right)* is seen in the photograph above inspecting troops of the French SAS towards the end of World War II. (IWM)

SAS soldiers working behind the lines with partisans would prominently display the British flag to notify Allied aircraft of their presence in the area. Exactly the same system was used during the Gulf War. This photograph was taken in Italy. (IWM)

Entry into the jungles of Malaya and Borneo was difficult, the quickest method being by parachute. This involved landing in the high jungle canopy and became known as tree-jumping. The technique was at best very dangerous, and those who survived the impact with the trees still had to lower themselves to the jungle floor. These SAS troops are preparing for a tree jump. Note the paniers on their right hips in the photo above. These contained the lines they used to lower themselves to the ground.

As the SAS established itself once more as a regular British unit, the tasks they were expected to undertake came thick and fast. Between 1959 and 1967, the SAS were active in Aden, Borneo and Oman. Here we see an SAS patrol being briefed in the jungle in Borneo before setting out on their mission.

With the increasing use of helicopters, tree-jumping declined, yet the conditions on the ground remained very much as they do today. This is one of the first pictures taken where helicopters were used for jungle insertion. (IWM)

In 1959 Jebel Akhdar in Oman was the scene for a daring SAS operation. Some 70 men from 'D' Squadron were transported directly from the jungle to the desert, where they immediately went into action. During the assault on Jebel Akhdar, a young captain by the name of Peter De la Billiere won the Military Medal for his actions. These photographs show the rugged terrain of the Jebel and riot training underway in the Jebeli village of Saiq.

The role of the SAS during the Aden conflict was limited to up-country patrolling and 'Keeni Meeni' (Swahili for snake in the grass) covert units mainly comprising of Fijians who operated in the towns, passing themselves off as Arabs. It was a conflict the SAS found difficult to come to grips with, partly due to the deteriorating political situation and the number of enemy factions involved. That said, they stayed to the bitter end and were involved in most of the action. This picture was taken during the massive riots in Crater district. The road in the centre was the only way into Crater. (IWM A 35119)

This SAS trooper is preparing his L42 sniper rifle prior to being lifted by helicopter into the mountains overlooking Crater. The local uprising had succeeded in killing most of the white population trapped in the area. Many of the bodies had been laid out in the road for the Arab trucks to run over. After the arrival of the SAS sniper group, the streets became deserted. (P)

CHAPTER TWO

SELECTION AND TRAINING

The SAS selection course takes place in the Brecon Beacons. The whole course has two aims, to weed out those who are unsuitable, and to push to the limit those capable of passing. The overall course, which was devised in the early 50s by Major John Woodhouse, has changed very little over the years, although more emphasis was placed on safety after a series of deaths in the late 70s and early 80s. The course is long and tough. Those who pass the build-up to test week find that at the end they are faced with the 'Endurance March'. Little can prepare them for this challenge - to succeed inside the allocated time is a fitting achievement in itself.

Continuation training lasts for fourteen weeks, at which time those candidates surviving selection will be taught all the basics that make a good SAS soldier. These include operating as a member of a four-man patrol and learning Standard Operating Procedures (SOPs). Specialist weapons skills and Combat Survival Training follow. The Combat Survival phase ends with an Escape and Evasion exercise, where candidates are expected to avoid capture. However, irrespective of capture, all candidates undergo intensive interrogation training.

Those remaining will go on to Jungle Training, and static-line parachuting. Even then, it is not finished. SAS candidates are required to swim at least a mile fully clothed, complete with belt equipment. Less demanding but equally essential is possession of a full driving licence. Only once the candidate has fulfilled all of the criterion required on the selection course will he be marched in to receive his beret with its coveted winged dagger. It bestows an ethos of belonging; a bond with those warriors who have gone before and given so much. Then he is sent to a Sabre Squadron as an SAS soldier.

SAS candidate checking his map. Try cheating and you are on your way out. Loads and distances will depend on the exercise, but the endurance march, or 'Fan Dance' as it is sometimes called, defies imagination.

The wild Brecon Beacons, home of the SAS basic training. This barren, exposed range of small mountains is, during bad weather, as hostile as any other place on earth. It has claimed the lives of many soldiers.

The basic rule of selection: pace yourself. Walk up the hill and run on the way down – this way you just might make the grade. Never stop and never give up.

Opposite top and bottom: Those who pass test week will go on to complete the fourteen-week continuation training. Here the individuals learn how to operate as a four-man patrol. Many of the soldiers come from infantry regiments, and normally their fieldcraft skills are excellent. Nevertheless, going back to the basics helps to bring everyone up to the same high standard. This four-man patrol is re-learning contact drills. (P)

Another priority in the SAS is surveillance. Staying concealed means choosing a good observation position (OP). Weapon sighting systems have become very sophisticated, and require expert knowledge. The value of the equipment a modern SAS soldier carries into battle totals many thousands of pounds, and it is generally state of the art. These pictures show a laser target designator (top), and a night vision aid (right), which allows the patrol to see perfectly during the dark hours. (P)

No matter what parent regiment you come from, basic skills must be re-learned. Weapon skills are a necessity and learning to strip, assemble and fire almost every type of weapon is taught, as these two pictures show. The machine guns are M60s and the small weapon is an Usi. Pictures taken around 1975. (P)

These soldiers are having a field day in more than one sense of the word, firing off a variety of weapons. The top picture shows the General Purpose Machine Gun (GPMG) in the sustained fire role. The bottom picture is of a fire power demonstration. (P)

Soldiers on basic static-line parachute training, taken inside a helicopter.
This picture was taken at the ILRRP (International Long Range
Reconnaissance Patrol) School, in Germany. Irrespective of location, all SAS
soldiers are expected to undergo several parachute jumps annually. (P)

Before any soldier can enter an SAS squadron, he must first pass the basic
parachute course. This picture was taken during a basic parachute course
at Brize Norton, and shows paratroopers dropping from a Hercules using
the new low-level parachute. The SAS now run their own specialist
parachute course. (PHOTO PRESS)

Target attack also plays a major role in the SAS. Despite the advent of Laser Target Designators (LTD), demolition skills are still required. These pictures show the demolition team fitting standard charges to an earth satellite station. (P)

Four months of intensive training make up the SAS demolition course, one of the most exciting courses in which a soldier can participate. (P)

The Laser Target Designator (LTD) has begun to play a major part in SAS training. The more traditional method of destroying a target by plastering it with explosive charges entailed carrying large amounts of explosive on to the target. Most vital installations are well protected, making it extremely difficult to get to the target, and there are the additional problems of being spotted while placing the charges or the charges being discovered before they have been detonated. The LTD simply allows the patrol to mark the target from a distance. A wide variety of smart bombs and cruise missiles fired from a safe distance can lock on to the laser 'painted' target. These two pictures were taken in Scotland. Note the Harrier coming in just above sea level. The LTD is the small device on the short legs. (P)

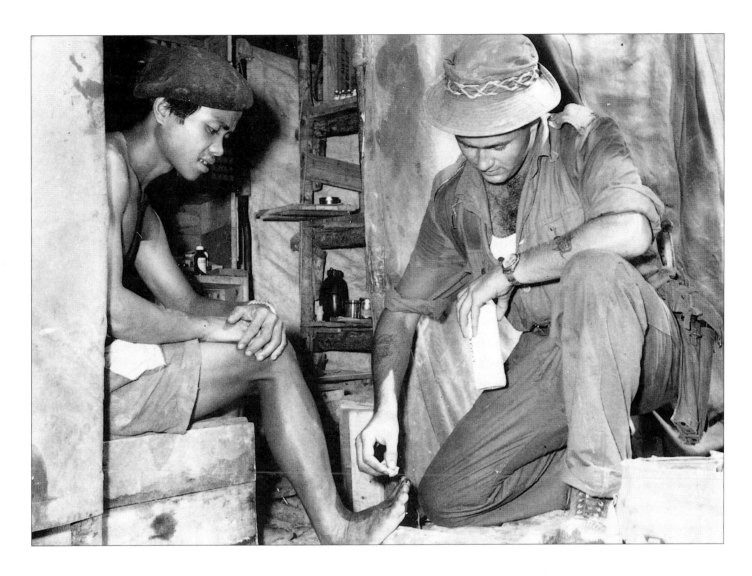

One in four SAS men is trained in medical skills. This is done to provide basic life-saving support on the battlefield until the casualty can be evacuated. Additionally, medical skills play a large part in any 'hearts and minds' campaign. The picture on the right was take in Oman, and shows a young boy with an infected leg. When the scab was removed it exposed the bone. Several weeks later, following a course of penicillin, he recovered, thanks to the SAS medic. The top picture is of an aborigine man being treated during an SAS patrol visit to a local campong in Malaya. (Soldier Mag)

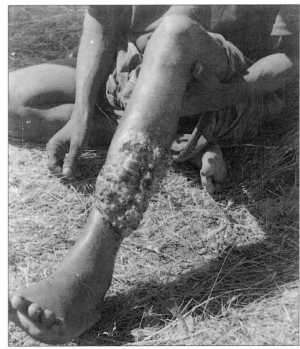

Almost every SAS soldier can speak at least one language other than his native tongue. Not everyone is your enemy, and the ability to converse is of immense help to the SAS while operating behind the lines. The soldier in this picture is explaining in Arabic that the tin of food contains no pork. A simple thing, but one that could cause major problems with a Muslim. This Arab is from a tribe named the Bani Shihoo, as indicated by the small axe he is holding. (P)

The communication skills in the SAS are second to none. Sophisticated field radios send burst-coded messages back to base in a matter of seconds. At one stage, the regiment had out-stations around the world that would transmit back to the Hereford base. With the advent of satellites, SAS communications are totally secure and operate direct on a global scale. Even in the deepest jungle, amid torrid downpours, the signaller has to get through. (P)

Jungle patrolling techniques differ from those in Europe. Here, not just the lead scout needs to be alert, but so do the rest of the patrol. This is an SAS lead scout on operation in South America. (P)

Jungle training comes at the end of selection and is something of a shock. Life in the jungle is different, especially the SAS way. Movement is slow, and there is no talking. The jungle soldier is always soaking wet, either from sweat or from the tropical rain. The base camp, where all the instruction is carried out, is normally nothing more than a few basic huts that the directing staff have thrown up. Everyone sleeps in a hammock under a basha. (P)

There is no need to starve in the jungle as it offers a bountiful supply of food, fresh water, and the means to build a good shelter. However, most of the insects and animals in the jungle will give you a nasty bite. This SAS soldier, while training in Belize, has built his basha high off the ground. Even his mug and boots are raised out of harm's way. (P)

The pictures on the left, (Soldier Mag) and above (P) show lead scouts operating in the jungles of South America. The soldier above is using a shotgun, often the preferred weapon of the lead scout.

The thickly matted jungle hides the sheer gradients and rugged terrain in which SAS soldiers must sometimes operate. Amid this tapestry of vibrant sounds and smells the four-man patrol finds itself in a murderous game of hide and seek. This patrol is about to cross a river. Note that they are using their bergens, wrapped in an air-tight sack, as floatation aids. (P)

Finding a landing zone for the helicopter is not always possible. These SAS soldiers are just about to repel into the jungle by rope. The versatility of the helicopter also makes it possible for injured soldiers to be winched from the jungle in an emergency. (P)

Due to the dense undergrowth and foliage, contact in the jungle is usually at short range. The ability to react with speed and aggression during an enemy ambush may well save your life. This picture shows an SAS man being put through his paces on a make-shift range. The weapon is an M16 with a 203 40mm grenade launcher. This picture was taken around 1988. (P)

These three photos were taken at the end of a Jungle Training exercise in Brunei in 1986. The helicopter coming in low over the tree-tops gives the waiting troops a real boost. Soon they'll be back in civilisation with real beds and dry clothes.

CHAPTER THREE

COMBAT SURVIVAL

The SAS regularly operate behind the enemy lines. It is what they started out doing, and what they do best. For this reason, Escape and Evasion Training plays a large part not only during selection, but also on an annual basis for members of the regiment. The psychological factors confronting the soldier when he is captured include pain, fatigue, boredom, loneliness, and the effects of cold. These symptoms, together with hunger and thirst, work to induce fear. SAS soldiers are taught to recognise the symptoms and understand their effects in the hope that they will defeat them.

The very nature of his predicament will fill the soldier's mind with a sense of isolation and abandonment. His captors may seek revenge by giving him a beating. From the moment of capture, the prisoner must be pre-

pared to encounter some hostility. In the eyes of his captors, he is the enemy personified and responsible for all the deeds carried out by his own forces. Combat Survival Training is designed to reproduce these conditions, stopping short of any physical injury.

Survival requires special skills, skills that have long been forgotten by those living in comfortable houses in civilised towns. Living off the land, lighting a fire without matches and finding your direction without a compass are just a few of the essential survival skills taught to the SAS soldier. The importance of a survival kit cannot be underestimated, and each SAS soldier on every operation will have his own survival kit with him. With this, and the aid of escape money or a 'blood chit', he will have the means to effect his escape, evade the enemy, and return safely to his own lines.

Four SAS men, all dressed in old army overcoats, are prepared for the Escape and Evasion exercise which comes at the end of selection. The regiment runs at least one E & E exercise every year. These soldiers will be on the run for about a week, living off the land whilst being pursued by a hunter force. Then they will face a forced interrogation. (P)

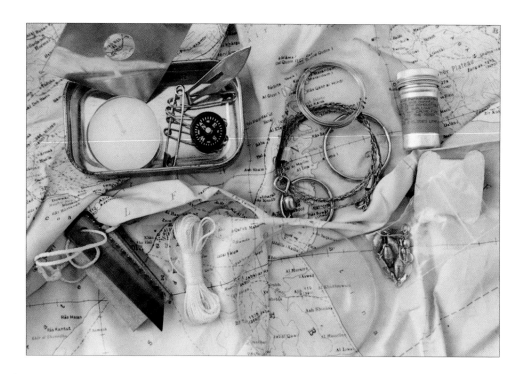

These essentials form part of an SAS escape kit, which is normally housed in a tobacco tin. The items can include: a button compass which can be swallowed; a wire saw that will cut through the hardest metal; a condom for collecting water, and a tampon for use in fire lighting. The magnesium block, bottom left, will light around 2000 fires, wet or dry. It is normally left to the individual soldier to prepare his own survival pack, as contents will depend on the operation and the environment. (P)

In addition to the basic survival items, specialist equipment is also issued. The picture below shows a cloth escape map, printed on silk, which was used during the Gulf War. Lock-picking tools are not issued for escape kits, but many SAS soldiers have acquired their own. The gold sovereigns are issued as 'blood money' with which the soldier can purchase assistance or equipment that will aid his escape. Most SAS soldiers operating behind the lines receive either gold or US dollars. (P)

SERIAL NO ....

PROMISORY NOTE

HM BRITANNIC GOVERNMENT PROMISES TO PAY THE BEARER OF THIS NOTE THE
SUM OF £5000 STERLING PROVIDING YOU DO NOT HARM THE PERSON ISSUING IT
AND THAT YOU ASSIST HIM TO EITHER EVADE CAPTURE OR RETURN HIM TO EITHER
SAUDI ARABIA OR TO NEUTRAL TERRITORY. TO CLAIM THE REWARD YOU SHOULD
TAKE THIS NOTE TO ANY BRITISH EMBASSY OR CONSULATE AND ASK TO SPEAK TO
THE DEFENCE ATTACHE OR ONE OF HIS ASSISTANTS. HE WILL THEN GIVE YOU THE
SUM OF £5000.

سند اذني

تتعهد الحكومة البريطانية بالدفع لحامل هذا السند الاذني مبلغ ٥٠٠٠ جنيه استرليني شرطاً
الا تضر الفرد المصدر له وشرطاً ان تساعده في تفادي الاسر او ان تقوم باعادته الى المملكة
العربية السعودية او الى ارض محايدة. من اجل اخذ المكافأة عليك تقديم هذا السند الى سفارة
او قنصلية بريطانية وطلب الالتقاء بالملحق الدفاعي او احد معاونيه. ثم سوف يعطى لك المبلغ
المحدد اي ٥٠٠٠ جنيه استرليني.

سند اذني

تتعهد الحكومة البريطانية بالدفع لحامل هذا السند الاذني مبلغ
٥٠٠٠ جنيه استرليني شرطاً الا تضر الفرد المصدر له وشرطاً
ان تساعده في تفادي الاسر او ان تقوم باعادته الى المملكة العربية
السعودية او الى ارض محايدة. من اجل اخذ المكافأة عليك
تقديم هذا السند الى سفارة او قنصلية بريطانية وطلب الالتقاء
بالملحق الدفاعي او احد معاونيه. ثم سوف يعطي لك المبلغ
المحدد اي ٥٠٠٠ جنيه استرليني.

The 'blood chit' is a document that the escaping soldier will
show to any civilian who agrees to help him. Each 'blood chit'
has a unique number at the top and any civilian who has aided
a soldier may approach any British Embassy or Consulate to
claim his reward. This 'blood chit' was issued for the Gulf War
and is in English, Arabic and Farsi. (P)

Living off the land is fast becoming a forgotten skill. Here the SAS 'survivor' is in training learning to tickle a trout. Below the survivor has successfully caught a rabbit, using a simple snare trap. Survival training also includes instruction on plant food recognition. (P)

Different countries will offer different game. This SAS soldier shot and ate a baboon while operating in central Africa. The whole patrol feasted well, as the meat is very tasty. (P)

The wild turkey was trapped during a Jungle Training exercise. It was full of fleas, but provided a good meal. (P)

Lighting a fire without matches is a skill most SAS men have learnt. When you are wet, cold and hungry, cooking your catch over an open fire will lift your spirits during any survival situation. (P)

Every SAS soldier soon learns that the weight of the kit he carries determines how fast and for how long he can keep moving. With this in mind, a simple condom can be used for collecting water. It is extremely light when empty but by placing it in a sock for support, the condom will hold about two litres of water. Filling the condom, however, is not as easy as it looks. (P)

A different water technique is shown here, as RAF Tornado pilots receive Desert Survival Training. The pilot has constructed a 'solar still'. This comprises of a polythene sheet stretched over a hole in the sand. The plastic sheet is weighted over a cup which collects the moisture that has condensed on the underside of the sheet. The pilot is sucking the water from beneath the sheet using a flexible tube. Fast jet pilots are normally instructed on survival through the ILRRP school in Southern Germany. (IWM)

Capture by the enemy can often seem very real during training. The use of unusual or 'enemy' uniforms by the hunter force adds to this realism as does the roughness with which the prisoner is treated. Some of these pictures were taken during the making of a film on SAS Escape and Evasion, and are very authentic. (P)

The captured SAS man can expect no sympathy from the enemy, so none is given during training. After a 24-hour period of interrogation, the prisoner really starts to think that he is in enemy hands. Capture and interrogation by the enemy is one of the most frightening experiences a soldier must face. SAS Combat Survival Training is designed to prepare the individual, should that day ever arrive. (P)

Torture during training is not allowed, but controlled applications of fear-inducing methods are used. White sound, and forcing the prisoner to wear a pillow case soaked with water, gives him the impression of slow drowning. It is an experience to be avoided. The basic rule is: give your name, rank and number only. Isolation will take up most of the 24 hours allocated to interrogation. During this time, the prisoner is kept constantly hooded, and normally housed in a cold, damp room. In reality, the prisoner is very uncomfortable, but the constant playing of white sound can cause hallucinations of warmth and sunshine. (P)

These pictures, taken during training, of an SAS escapee attacking a guard are very real. Note the speed of movement of the SAS man. (P)

After knocking the unfortunate guard unconscious, the SAS man is gone, leaving nothing more than a blur. (The above two photographs were taken at normal speed, without any special effects.) (P)

The enemy will not give up without a chase. Here the escaping soldier is forced to jump into the river, a drop of some 40 feet. He then has to swim the river fully clothed, something he would have learnt during his selection course. (P)

Rescue at last. This escapee has finally managed to make contact with friendly forces and is about to be picked up by helicopter. He has adopted the crucifix position, facing away from the helicopter, so that they can see that he poses no threat to them. This picture was taken recently, during the making of a Combat Survival film. (P)

CHAPTER FOUR

TROOP TRAINING

The SAS is made up of four Sabre (fighting) Squadrons. Each squadron is sub-divided into four troops with a small headquarters section. Each troop is designed to operate in a variety of terrains and environments, providing different methods of delivering soldiers to their drop-off points. These include vehicle mobility, mountaineering and Arctic warfare, air insertion and boat entry methods. Each troop member will have an individual skill, ranging from medical training to languages, demolition and signals. These are the basic skills and, depending on their length of service, it is not uncommon to find a troop member with several different skills. Additionally, each troop will specialise in its own unique skills.

Mountain Troop is responsible for all aspects of mountaineering and skiing. New members with no previous experience will be taught the basics of climbing and Arctic tactics. Many SAS individuals attend courses in Europe, among the best of which is the German Alpine Guides course. Normally, one of the squadrons will be committed to the NATO winter exercise in Norway.

Boat Troop concentrates on all water insertion methods. These include diving and even swimming ashore on a surf board. In recent years, members of the SBS (Special Boat Service) have been stationed at Hereford and join with the SAS in cross-training. Several operations have been jointly carried out using the SBS for actual water insertion and during the Falklands War they demonstrated how truly professional they are.

Every SAS soldier is required to be parachute trained before he can enter a squadron. Air-Insertion Troop extends beyond these normal static-line procedures and practises HAHO (High Altitude High Opening). This allows the men to glide some 30 kilometres on to a target. Air-Insertion Troop also uses unusual entry methods including micro-lights and power-kites.

Mobility Troop operates using a wide variety of vehicles, of which the SAS 'Pink Panther' or 'Pinkie' is best known. The regiment decided to paint their vehicles pink when an old aircraft, shot down during World War II, was found in the middle of the desert - the sand had burnished it pink. Other vehicles used by Mobility Troop include KTM 350 and Honda 250 motorbikes; the Honda is preferred as it is very quiet. Courses for members of Mobility Troop cover several weeks with the REME learning basic mechanical fault finding and training in cross-country conditions.

An SAS diver has to be ready to operate the moment he is ashore. This soldier is taking part in an anti-terrorist exercise in 1995. (P)

Boat Troop deals with all water-borne entry methods. These two men are paddling a 'Klepper' canoe. The canoe is basically a canvas cover over a wooden frame, allowing it to be dismantled and stowed away. It can be launched from a submarine. (P)

Inside the pool at Stirling Lines in Hereford. This picture shows the indoor water facility which can simulate various conditions for boat and diving work. The pool is fitted with a wave-making machine, generating rough sea conditions.

Fast patrol boats are used by the SAS for their speed and manoeuvrability.

When swimming ashore, equipment can be kept dry inside specially designed waterproof bags. (P)

A more dramatic entry can be made by dropping from a helicopter. This picture captures the moment a diver launches himself into the water. Over the years, many different entry methods had been tried, including firing divers from the torpedo tube of a submarine. Not something for those who suffer from claustrophobia. (P)

All members of Mountain Troop are required to undergo a basic climbing course. These new recruits are practising on the walls of Llanberris Pass in North Wales. During the summer months, climbing like this can be great fun and very satisfying. (P)

Members of Mountain Troop expand their skills by training overseas. This picture was taken at the French Military Climbing School at Chamonix. All the men in the pictures are SAS soldiers, and their climbing ability is clear to see. (P)

The SAS produces men of outstanding talent. This picture is of Andy Baxter, climbing during a training exercise in Southern Germany. Like Brummie Stokes and Bronco Lane before him, Andy went on to tackle Mount Everest. Unfortunately, he was badly injured during an avalanche, and died some months later. His skill and dedication to mountaineering were second to none. As a young SAS soldier, Andy excelled at almost everything he did. His love of climbing came after attending the German Alpine Guides course in Bavaria. The regiment annually selects two Mountain Troop soldiers to attend the year-long course. Six months is spent on skiing and six on mountaineering. In many ways, Andy Baxter epitomised the daring spirit of the SAS – always first to rise to a challenge, and meet that challenge with skill and daring.

Mountain Troop also specialises in skiing, most of which is carried out in Norway. Basic skiing is a requirement for all SAS soldiers, and during any training it falls to Mountain Troop to supply the expertise. Basic skiing is a very casual affair, as can be seen by the mixed dress in this picture.

To improve the standards of skiing, a weekly race is run. The course distance increases as the training continues. Many individuals become highly competitive, and go on to compete in races against other armies.

The SAS practise their military role in Norway. This normally means living in a snow hole for weeks at a time and observing the enemy. As with many SAS operations, intelligence gathering is a prime role. This picture was taken from an SAS snow hole, while overlooking the 'enemy' encampment below. (P)

Many operations are carried out using vehicles, and Mobility Troop utilises a wide range of vehicles, from Land Rovers to motorbikes. The SAS 'Pink Panther' is recognised world-wide, and has become a trademark of the SAS. The current vehicle is the 110 Land Rover. This comes fitted with a variety of armaments, and is adapted to suit most terrains. However, the vehicle in this picture is in need of a little help, and is being winched from the mud by a sister vehicle. (P)

Although they work in groups, most of the Land Rovers can operate independently. Understandably, skills such as navigation are a basic requirement. Here the crew are using a theodolite to fix their position. Despite the use of modern Global Plotting Systems (GPS), the more traditional skills are still practised. (P)

Mobility Troop operates in all terrains. This picture was taken during a river crossing in the African bush. Training in cross-country conditions can vary from the UAE (United Arab Emirates) to the deserts of America. (P)

Mobility Troop also needs to be familiar with vehicles not normally associated with the SAS. Training with other units of the British Army allows them access to, for example, the Scorpion tank. (P)

Joint training between the various troops also takes place. These pictures show Mobility Troop negotiating a ride on a Boat Troop rigid raider. The small vehicle is a Honda 350 Quad. (P)

Getting ready for a high-altitude jump, the men will move from the main oxygen control panel to their personal supply. (Photo Press)

There is an Air Insertion Troop with each squadron, normally referred to as the 'Prima Donnas'. Their tasks are more individual, as they are normally only involved with the rest of the squadron in the path-finding role, going in ahead of the main force to secure and mark a drope zone or landing area. Every SAS soldier, when he has finished selection, will attend the SAS parachute course. This involves four low-altitude (200ft) static line jumps, seven normal (800ft) jumps and two water jumps. Here the SAS soldier is fully rigged out for a high-altitude jump, complete with oxygen system. (Photo Press)

Exiting the aircraft and going into the 'delta' position. Note the rucksacks are secured, upside down, on the soldiers' backside. When the parachute has opened, the equipment is lowered away from the body on a rope.

After a hard day's training, whether jumping, swimming, driving, climbing or skiing, there's nothing like a nice cold beer.

CHAPTER FIVE

OMAN

The Oman War was one the British public knew little about. It was a war of counter-insurgency against communist-backed rebels and a war that took the lives of many good SAS men. The country itself is rich in oil and its northern tip controls the Straits of Hormuz, through which half the world's oil passes. The country prior to 1970 was as backward as any third world nation. A feudal state where the people lived without progress or the hope of change, rebellion in the region was rife. The situation was saved when the regime of Said bin Taimur was deposed by his son Qaboos in a bloodless coup.

The young Sultan declared a general amnesty, and put into progress plans that would bring his people out of the dark ages. This pledge of social development won many of the people over to the government, but there were a great many hard-line communists who resisted. Almost immediately, two squadrons of the SAS were moved into the area, where they remained for several years, officially known as the British Army Training Team (BATT). During the long war, many battles were fought and of these the Battle of Mirbat must rank as the greatest. At dawn on the 19th of July, 1972, a large rebel force, about 250 strong, attacked the Port of Mirbat in the Dhofar Province of Southern Oman.

When the battle started, Corporal Labalaba and trooper Takavesi, both members of a nine-man Special Air Service Civil Action team, went to man a 25-pounder gun just outside the walls of the fort, north-west of the town. Gunner Walid Khalfan of the Oman Artillery was already there. Before long the entire crew were wounded. The rebels continued to attack with great ferocity and made repeated attempts to take the gun, often from within grenade-throwing range, and despite the supporting fire from the other Special Air Service soldiers. The action lasted nearly four hours before a relief force and an accompanying air strike drove off the enemy. During this action Corporal Labalaba was killed, Trooper Tobin fatally injured and Trooper Takavesi and Gunner Walid Khalfan both seriously wounded.

When the war was won, the civil aid teams moved in. They drilled for water, and for the first time this precious liquid was plentiful. Bulls were imported and the local herds were improved, bringing better food to the population. The SAS were fully involved with these efforts, working with the local people not just to fight off the rebels, but also to improve the basic standard of living.

Today, the reforms instigated by Sultan Qaboos have brought Oman into the modern world, with good schools, roads and hospitals, a far cry from the bad old days of the 60s.

The Jebel Massive is a strange place to fight a war. In places it is cut with steep sided gorges that are reminiscent of the Grand Canyon. To the north, the vegetation fades out to nothing, only rock and sand. To the east and west, buried in the gorges, small villages have developed terraced fields. To the south, the Jebel Massive drops away sharply to the Indian Ocean. In the greener regions, it is a place of great beauty. Birds nest in the trees and wild animals can be spotted on the slopes. (P)

The local Jebelis were a proud people, existing on the very basics of life, which in many cases, meant little more than surviving. They had lived this way for thousands of years, building houses of stone, constructing cisterns in the rock to catch water and breeding cattle for food. Many of the young men travelled throughout the Middle East, some in search of work, some just wishing to expand their minds. On returning to their own miserable living conditions, having seen the way that people lived in other countries, it is little wonder that they revolted. (P)

Opposite: Sultan Qaboos, ruler of Oman. His father, Sultan Said bin Taimur, kept the country in a backward, feudal manner. Then, in 1970, Qaboos, who had been trained at the British Military Academy in Sandhurst, deposed his father in a bloodless coup at the Palace. Since that time he has employed all his energies to improve his country and help his people. (Frank Spooner)

One of the first tasks that the SAS had to deal with was to inform the local population about the palace coup and the intentions of their new leader, Qaboos. This picture was taken by the medical tent that had been set up at the start of a hearts and minds campaign. The men were given small portable radios, while the children were given T-shirts. (P)

These Jebeli children are holding leaflets announcing that Sultan Qaboos is their new ruler. The leaflets were provided by the SAS Psychological Warfare Team. (P)

In the north of Oman, the only way to visit some of the coastal villages was by boat. The Trucial Oman Scouts crewed this Arab dhow, which spent a month going around the isolated villages. This picture shows the dhow leaving a small cove, inland from the sea. Here the SAS party found several families which had been banished under the old Sultan's rule. They had survived for years on brackish water and fish from the sea. (P)

This picture shows the town of Taqa. It lies between the southern capital Salalah, and the town of Mirbat. The old fort housed the local Wali and his soldiers, and directly opposite is the house used for many years by the SAS. The tree indicates the centre of the town square. Just a few years before the SAS arrived, slaves were still sold in this square. Taqa was constantly under enemy fire prior to the SAS assaulting the Jebel Massive. (P)

This Arab builder had fallen off a roof a week before the SAS dhow arrived. The hole in his skull was plastered with a mixture of dates and salt. To some extent this treatment had worked, but when the SAS medic removed the makeshift poultice, a large square of skull came away with it. This hole, with the brain in full view, caused a problem. Eventually, the medic opened a ration pack and cut the lid off a metal can of processed cheese. He sterilised the lid by boiling it, and secured it over the hole with some decorative stitching. The man was given antibiotics and on the next visit a month later, the wound had almost healed. The letters 'ese' on the tin lid could still be seen, but with time that would heal over. (P)

The Adoo (Arabic for enemy) were mostly conscripted from the local Jebelis. They were fast, could live off the land, and knew where every water hole was located. In the early years, it was difficult to come to grips with them and they were free to roam the Jebel Massive, attacking the coastal towns at will. (P)

Things soon changed when the SAS led their Firqats (indigenous forces trained by the SAS, many of whom had previously fought for the Adoo) into the fray. These three Adoo were killed during one of the first contacts on the Jebel. Normally the Adoo were well dressed, fighting in green shorts and shirts. Around their waists were ammunition belts and *The Thoughts of Chairman Mao* was always kept in a handy pocket. In fairness, they were a brave adversary, fighting for a misguided cause. (P)

Not a pretty picture. After a major stand-off attack a patrol was sent out to see what damage had been caused. A mortar bomb had landed amid a group of Adoo, killing many of them instantly. When the mortar controller asked for a body count, the patrol member reported, 'Four plus an odd arm.' Nothing else of the guy could be found. (P)

The British Army Training Team, or BATT as they were known, played a major part in the Oman War. Without their contribution, the war may not have been won. This picture shows a typical group of SAS BATT. (P)

Once the running battles were over, the BATT settled down into fire-bases. These were easier to re-supply, and a build-up of stores was possible. The bases were all well defended, usually by building sandbagged bunkers around the perimeter fence that protected the heli-pad or air-strip. (P)

Defending the locations against Adoo stand-off attacks was mainly down to the GPMGs and mortars. At times, to cover more long-range patrols, the Omani artillery would supply a field gun and crew. (P)

Always ready, the SAS mortar men would live, eat, and sleep in the mortar pit. It was a challenge for them to listen out for the Adoo mortars being fired, and then get rounds in the air before the enemy bombs had landed. (P)

The two SAS soldiers in this picture are posing in a disused mortar pit. The Adoo scored a bulls-eye when one of their mortar rounds landed right on target. By a stroke of sheer luck, the mortar was unmanned at the time. (P)

Author's Note: This was a day to remember! We had won this fire-base only after a fierce battle with the Adoo the previous night. About an hour after I took this picture, one of our patrols, some 2000 metres to the front, came under heavy fire. I was part of a relief group sent out to provide the retreating patrol with covering fire. During a fire fight, I was shot in the leg no more than 300 metres from this location - I was lucky, the guy next to me was hit in the heart. (P)

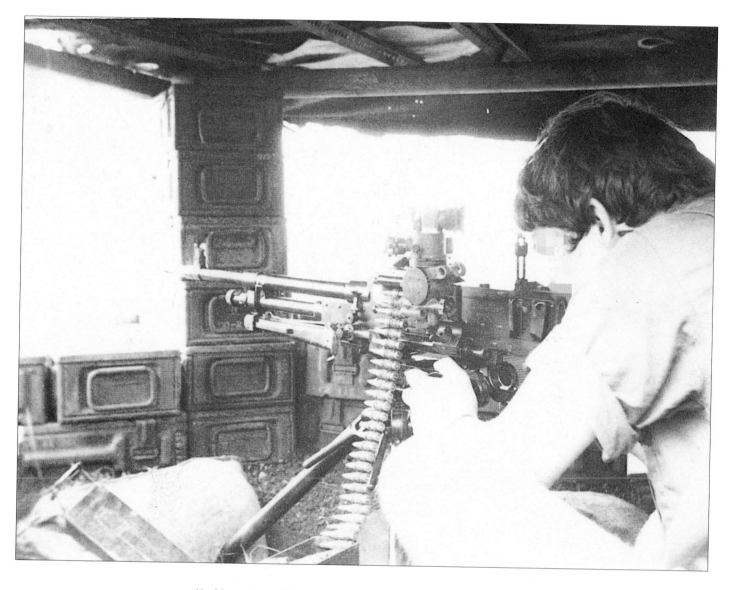

Machine-gun positions were often constructed from old
ammunition boxes. The firepower and reliability of the GPMG
played a major part in the successful outcome of the conflict. (P)

Opposite: During the monsoon season, this was home. The mist
came in and the drizzle started, and no one moved. There was no
re-supply, as the choppers could not fly. There was very little
action, as the Adoo could not stand the wet and cold either. For
the SAS it was a matter of putting up with the mud and burying
their heads in a good book. This picture is more reminiscent of
the Somme than the Middle East. (P)

From the firm fire-bases, the fighting patrols would go hunting. Some patrols would move in the daytime, but night operations were preferred. This picture shows the SAS in rehearsal for a large ambush on the border with Yemen. (P)

After being choppered in close to the Yemeni border, the SAS ambush would sweat out the daylight hours using what cover they could. The heat during the day was unbearable, but at night, while waiting in the ambush position, it was freezing. (P)

The Sultan of Oman's Air-Force, (SOAF) was, during the campaign, manned mainly by European pilots. They were exceptionally good, and would do everything in their power to assist the BATT. From the start, the helicopters (Hueys) were in constant use; they were needed to ferry troops, evacuate the wounded, and supply ammunition and water. (P)

As the serviceable hours of the helicopters ticked away, the SAS were forced to build air-strips on which the Shorts Skyvan could land. It made sense, as the Skyvan could bring in a much larger load. However, sometimes the SAS would have to fight for a location, defend it and build an air-strip all in the same night. In fairness to the Skyvan pilots, they would land on anything the SAS constructed. Equally, the Skyvan itself proved to be a major asset in winning the all-important logistical war. (P)

The SOAF Strikemaster. These neat little fighter aircraft were combat
models of the Gnat trainer. As the Adoo had little or no air support, the
Strikemasters made a big difference to any battle. During the battle for
Mirbat, had it not been for the SOAF jets coming in at low altitude and
stopping the Adoo on the wire perimeter, then the outcome would have
been very different. (P)

As the war came to an end, the Adoo retreated to a cave complex in the Shirshitti wadi. These caves were said to hold tons of weapons, food and combat supplies. It was believed that their capture would help bring an end to the war. The task was given to the SAF (Sultan's Armed Forces) Jebel Regiment but, as always, the SAS and Firqat were involved. By mid-afternoon they had managed to reach a clearing called Point 985, whereupon a base was established. During the night the Adoo attacked at very close range, killing four members of the SAF and severely wounding many more. (P)

Next day the force advanced down into the Shirshitti. By mid-morning, Red Company had reached the Shirshitti wadi, but the commander realised that he had moved too far south. At this stage most of the SAS men had attached themselves to the various command headquarters. With Red Company was Lance Corporal Thomas. As the lead platoons broke cover (against the advice of Corporal Thomas) into an area clear of bush, the Adoo opened fire. Within seconds most of the platoon were dead, cut down by the ferocious Adoo fire-power. The Company Commander, together with several other men, rushed forward to get a better look at the situation. The Adoo had been waiting, and they too were cut down. Even to the hardened SAS men, the situation was clearly out of control. As in all such circumstances, the SAS quickly grouped together for support. All around them, those SAF soldiers that were still alive dropped their weapons and ran. This did not include the white officers, who tried desperately, sometimes at the cost of their own lives, to regain control. Order was eventually restored at gun point. As the shaken troops made their way back to Point 985, shots could be heard coming from down in wadi; the Adoo were confirming their kill. To alleviate this gruesome sound, a full-blown mortar barrage was called down on the battle area. These two pictures show the SAS men at dawn. They had been under attack all that night, sometimes from just a few metres.

This SAS patrol have located an enemy weapons cave. The inset picture shows some of the heavy weapons captured, covered in rust from storage in the damp caves. Throughout the Oman War the Adoo had a plentiful supply of weapons, most of which were transported in from neighbouring Yemen.

Once the main battles were over, and the areas were stabilised, civil aid teams were brought in. One of their first tasks was to exploit the vast underground sources of fresh water. This simple act played a major role in winning the hearts and minds campaign, as water had always been in short supply previously. The top picture clearly shows the water gushing from the ground, and flooding the desert. A new cattle breeding farm was set up to improve the large stock of cows on the Jebel Massive. Unfortunately, the Hereford bulls, imported from England, were too fit and heavy for the native beasts, and many would simply collapse under the bulls' weight. Eventually a metal frame was constructed to support the bull, the cows were backed in underneath the frame to be serviced. The SAS were fully involved in securing the sites for the water-drilling teams and helping in the cattle round-up. (P)

Many good SAS men died in the Oman War, and many others were badly wounded. This picture is of 'Gordie' Barker who, having fought through most of the battles, was killed in a parachuting accident. The smile that warms his face in this photograph is reminiscent of Gordie's good humour. On a typical day in Oman, Gordie would entertain the rest of the group by shaving them with a cut-throat razor. While doing this, endless jokes would abound, adding to the general comradeship.

CHAPTER SIX

NORTHERN IRELAND

Northern Ireland and the SAS did not make a particularly good combination. SAS soldiers were first deployed in the province in August 1969 when they openly patrolled the streets and manned road blocks wearing ordinary uniform including their own sand-coloured berets. Their tour of duty was brought to an end when it was decided that their specialist skills could be put to better use in Oman. It was not until 1974, when the situation in Northern Ireland had deteriorated considerably, that the SAS were sent back in.

Second time round, their role took on a more clandestine nature. Their own berets were seldom seen on the streets, with SAS soldiers adopting the colours of whichever regiment was officially resident in the border area. Eventually, they took on a completely covert role, patrolling the border in South Armagh and seeking out members of the IRA. Working from intelligence supplied by their own surveillance operations, or by any one of the confusion of other 'competing' intelligence agencies operating in the province, they became the strike force sent in to finish off the job. Even this role diminished somewhat, however, when units such as E4A (an undercover surveillance team made up of RUC Special Branch trained in Hereford by the SAS) developed the experience and aptitude to handle such tasks.

Surveillance, both static and mobile, formed a large part of SAS life in Northern Ireland and the conditions under which they had to work were difficult to say the least. The rules of contact gave away the edge, that element of surprise and swift action, that was the SAS stock in trade. Indeed, the rules of engagement often put soldiers in grave danger. Even when confronted by a member of the IRA carrying a bomb or gun, they were required to give the warning 'Stop or I shoot' - repeated three times. Inevitably, in a situation fraught with political complexities, SAS actions which led to shots being fired and people being killed caused an uproar with the IRA complaining of wholesale slaughter and the authorities trying to cover up in order to protect sensitive operations.

In a war which the regiment neither sought nor needed, and working under strict political supervision, they gave their best. From the moment the SAS entered the fray, the IRA death toll quickly rose. Their presence in Northern Ireland was, and still remains, a major deterrent to the terrorists.

This cross marks the spot where Gerard Martin and Brian Mullan were shot by the SAS. They had been involved in an action by the IRA when a bomb was detonated beneath a bus filled with members of the 1st Battalion The Light Infantry. Some ten days later, members of the IRA ASU (Active Service Unit) who had been responsible, crossed back into the north in order to attack another target. On 30 August 1988, the intended target, a policeman, was replaced by four SAS men. The SAS drove the intended target's Leyland truck to this site and faked a breakdown. The IRA appeared in a stolen car and opened fire - the SAS responded, killing the terrorists. (P)

An amazing shot of four members of the IRA who have just been firing at the security forces. Normally such incidents were hit-and-run tactics, but it is clear to see that the firing party have cover from the man crouching behind the wall. (IWM)

In the early 1970s the SAS would normally patrol with other units of the British army. This gave them an insight into the general situation and how the other ground forces operated in South Armagh. This picture of a Devon and Dorset Regiment patrol was taken in the market square of Crossmaglen. (Photo Press)

Bessbrook Mill, which has been in use since the start of the troubles, is still in use today. It is the main support base for troops working out of Forkhill and Crossmaglen. Every patrol must be inserted and re-supplied by helicopter. This puts a great strain on the RAF and Army Air Corps. This picture was taken in June 1996.

Two SAS men relaxing in the SAS bar in Bessbrook. Bessbrook was the home of the SAS in Northern Ireland for many years. Taken around 1976, note the long hair and scruffy appearance of the men in this photo. The SAS often had to try to pass themselves off as local workmen.

Captain Bob Nairac was killed by the IRA in Northern Ireland in May 1977. Although not a member of the SAS, Nairac did live and work out of the same location in Bessbrook, South Armagh. He was from a unit known as 14 Intelligence and Security, a covert unit used to gather information on which the SAS could then take action. A highly intelligent man, and certainly enormously courageous, Bob Nairac decided to visit a local pub close to the border with the Irish Republic. It was here that Nairac inadvertently drew attention to himself. As he attempted to leave and make his way back to the car park, he was followed. A fist fight pursued (Bob Nairac was an excellent boxer and could take care of himself) but during the tussle his Browning 9mm pistol fell to the ground. His assailants grabbed it and he was soon overpowered. Blindfolded and gagged, Nairac was taken by car to a field on the border where IRA members took control. He was interrogated and tortured in the corner of a field, using a fence post with which they beat him repeatedly around the body and head. Despite what has been called a murderous beating by the IRA themselves, Bob Nairac did not talk. In the end, they shot him with his own pistol and his body was disposed of, never to be recovered.

A farmer cutting his ditches discovered the path of a command wire leading to a large IRA bomb placed in a culvert beneath the main road. The SAS did a reconnaissance and discovered the firing point and the bomb. The picture indicates the path of the command wire to the bomb. In order to deactivate the bomb, the Ammunitions Technical Officer (ATO) was taken to the site by an SAS soldier and allowed to disarm the device. As the ATO did so, he stepped on a home-made pressure plate booby trap. He did not discover this until he had neutralised the bomb. Lucky for him, the pad between the pressure plates was thick enough to bear his weight. Had he been just a little heavier, he would have been blown to bits. Later, it took several drinks in the bar to stop the man from shaking.

Behind the picture of this SAS man playing the hunchback of Notre Dame, there is a very funny story, which in itself depicts the hardships that working in an observation position can bring. Two men had been sent out to observe and photograph a local barber's shop. The barber was suspected of being a member of the IRA, and pictures were required to establish who was visiting the premises. Eventually, the two men found a location for their OP in the ceiling of the town hall. Working in the space between the inner ornate roof and that of the buildings outer roof, the two men set up camp in the tiny maintenance space behind the town hall clock. At each side of the clock, through which was a sloping vent, clear pictures could be taken of the barber's shop across the street. Hot soup and sandwiches were delivered to the men during the early morning hours via a small trap door in the town hall ceiling. Messages, exposed film and waste were lowered down, with fresh supplies being hauled up. A bin liner placed in the gloom at the end of the catwalk which ran the length of the domed inner roof served as a toilet. The weather was very sunny and after about five days, the heat which became trapped between the inner and outer roofs was unbearable. One of the soldiers, in need of the toilet, worked his way along the catwalk towards the bag. Halfway along, he stopped, shocked by something moving in the gloom. There in front of him was the biggest spider man had ever seen. Its body was two feet across, and large eyes glistened in its head. The SAS man panicked, daring not to move for fear that it would attack him. Several moments went by before he realised that spiders that size do not exist. Then he saw what it was. The black bin liner had been twisted and sealed up with an elastic band after use, to cut down on the smell. As the heat had increased, the gases had expanded, creating a look-alike giant spider lurking in the half-light. With some relief, and fearing that the bag might explode at any moment, the SAS soldier committed a second error; he opened the sack. The smell hit him like a sledgehammer. He managed to crawl back to where his partner was keeping watch, only to find him face up against the vent trying to suck in clean air. Although funny, this story demonstrates the daily hardships that SAS men encounter in the war against terrorism - they stayed in the location undetected for three weeks. (P)

On the afternoon of 2 May, 1980, two cars sped down the Antrim Road deploying an SAS team to round up suspects from number 69. Another car covered the rear of the house. Unknown to the SAS, the IRA had mounted an American M60 machine gun in the upstairs window of the adjoining house. Captain Richard Westmacott, the commander of the mission, was sitting in the middle in the rear of one of the cars, and was the last to leave the vehicle. He was shot dead by a burst from the M60. Knowing that their officer was dead, the SAS men continued the assault until a white flag signalled the terrorists' surrender. The surrender was honoured. Captain Westmacott had joined the SAS from the Grenadier Guards and was an officer in 'G' Squadron. He was the first SAS soldier to be killed by the IRA. He did not personify the typical SAS officer – his fair, curly hair gave him the look of a schoolboy, and he had a love of poetry. But that was the surface. Inwardly, he was as tough as they come; he was awarded a posthumous Military Cross. His death ended the run of bad luck that had dogged the SAS in Northern Ireland, as three days later the boys stormed the Iranian Embassy in London. (P)

When the police station at Loughall was attacked by two active service units of the IRA, they were met with the full force of the SAS. It started when masked men stole a Toyota van from Dungannon. It was suspected that the van would be used in an attack. Surveillance by E4A had identified the target as Loughall. At a little past 7pm, the blue Toyota van drove down the road past the police station. It shortly returned from the direction of Portadown, this time followed by a JCB, in the cab where three hooded IRA terrorists. Declan Arthurs was driving, with Michael Gormley and Gerald O'Callaghan riding shotgun. The bucket was filled with explosive contained in an oil drum. While the blue van charged past the station, the JCB slammed through the gate. One of the two IRA men riding shotgun ignited the bomb. Back at the van, several hooded men jumped out and opened fire in the direction of the RUC station. At this stage the ambush was activated. All eight members of the IRA fell, hit by the devastating SAS fire. At the height of the fire-fight, the bomb exploded, taking with it half the RUC station. Without doubt, Loughall was one of the most successful operations ever mounted against the IRA, who were totally stunned by the loss of two complete active units. This is all that was left of the van. The rods indicate bullet holes. (Photo Press)

An SAS patrol being inserted for an operation in South Armagh. Their use in the province has always been highly publicised. At the time this picture was taken, the SAS would only fly in directly from Hereford dealing with a specific task. (P)

This picture shows the basic equipment carried by the SAS in
Northern Ireland. (P)

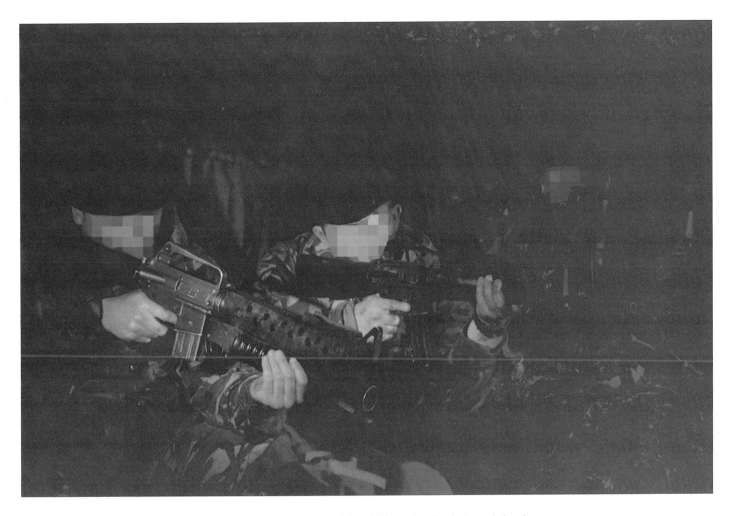

SAS men in an Observation Position (OP) on the South Armagh border. These two had just heard shots fired from a car, and the car then drove up to within a few metres of their location. The four people – two men and two women – then started to have sex. As the car rocked, the SAS men pounced, opening the car doors to reveal some very surprised faces. (P)

Much of the work in Northern Ireland is carried out at night. This soldier is about to leave his hide and patrol on to his target. (P)

One of the best attributes of the SAS is their ability to hide during daylight hours. But living in the ground is extremely uncomfortable. The lines on this photograph indicate the water levels of day one and day two, in the OP where this soldier was lying.

Although most people would regard the IRA as the enemy in Northern Ireland, the SAS, like the rest of the British Army presence in the province, were essentially there to keep the peace and could not afford to take sides. There are many instances when the SAS mounted operations against, for example, the Ulster Defence Association. One such incident involved Republican activist and former MP, Bernadette McAliskey (nee Devlin). Intelligence indicated that the Ulster Defence Association (UDA) planned to kill McAliskey together with her husband, Michael, at their isolated farmhouse near Coalisland on 16 January 1981. The SAS put the house under observation but the nearest they could conceal themselves was some 200 metres from the building. When the three gunmen arrived by car, they did so at speed, driving directly to the house. The SAS team responded immediately, but by the time they reached the house, the UDA had smashed the door in and shots were heard. The gunmen were arrested as they made their escape and on checking inside the house, the soldiers found Michael McAliskey bleeding from a severed artery and in a grave condition. Bernadette, although shot several times, was not so critical. The SAS medic kept them both alive until an ambulance arrived. The McAliskeys survived and the three UDA assassins were sentenced to between fifteen years and life imprisonment.

CHAPTER SEVEN

ANTI-TERRORIST TEAM

Much has been written about the SAS and their role in the anti-terrorist war. This role is characteristic of the modern SAS image and is certainly the area of operation that grabs the most media coverage. Governments began to look seriously at ways of combating the new breed of terrorism after the atrocity at the Munich Olympics in 1972. At the international G7 talks which followed, the heads of government made a secret pact to build up dedicated domestic forces capable of dealing with any terrorist situation, and to co-operate with each other in their training and operations.

In Britain, the SAS was given the task of equipping and training the new force that was to become the anti-terrorist team. The concept of combating people who would gladly risk their own lives to further their cause required a fresh approach right from the start. The equipment was new, the tactics were new and the SAS responded to the training with unmatched enthusiasm.

Today, the SAS provides the best anti-terrorist team in the world. Its techniques and equipment have been tried and tested in operations ranging from the Lufthansa airliner hijack in Mogadishu in 1977 to the Iranian Embassy siege in London in 1980. These special skills have been exported and used to train anti-terrorist teams of many other nations. The photographs used in this chapter help to underline the huge role played by the SAS in countering the internal and international terrorist threat.

The basic SAS anti-terrorist soldier standing outside the famous 'Killing House'. He is dressed in fire-retardant overalls and body armour. His head is protected with a flash hood and he is wearing a respirator with night goggles. The MP5 machine pistol is fitted with a torch, and his back-up weapon is a Browning 9mm Hi-Power pistol. Two stun grenades can be seen on his waist. (1990) (P)

The basic anti-terrorist team consists of about 30 men, although for operations this will vary depending on the situation. The men normally drive to the scene of the incident in Range Rovers and Transit vans, carrying with them the weaponry and equipment to go into action the moment they are on site. (1992) (P)

The 'Killing House' is the name given to a flat-roofed block building in the grounds of the Hereford base. It is one of the few buildings on the base that is in constant use. It was designed with the express purpose of perfecting individual shooting skills and building clearance drills practised by the SAS. The internal layout allows for many different scenarios, from simple target practice to room combat. Despite the millions of rounds that have been fired since the 'Killing House' was constructed and the realistic conditions under which training is carried out, there has to this day only been one fatality. The man who died was Ray Abbots (pictured above). Ray was a real character in the regiment. His love/hate relationship with certain members of the Signals Squadron was a constant source of amusement and his untimely death came as a great shock to everyone.

Author's Note: Ray was a bit of a loner, but he frequently came to dinner at my house, and spent several Christmases with my family. Beneath his stern exterior beat a heart of gold and he was a first-class soldier and a worthy friend.

Once at the incident site, the SAS may move into a nearby
holding area were they can be briefed and make preparations.
Heavier and more specialised equipment is carried in a large
box-van. (1982) (P)

Weapons will depend on the situation, but the MP5 and the MP5K (short) together with the stun grenades are almost always used. The stun grenades will momentarily blind, deafen and disorientate the targets, giving the SAS a precious few seconds to burst into the building. (1990) (P)

Opposite top and bottom: Training for the assault teams starts with basic room combat, working in two pairs of two, and involves all types of terrorist situation. Here the SAS can be seen storming a building using a vehicle and helicopter. Those on the roof are preparing to descend by rope, while those on the vehicle are using fixed ladders to gain entry. All the assault vehicles are fitted with special platforms enabling men, equipment and assault ladders to be carried outside the vehicle should it be necessary. (1985) (P)

As most hijackings or kidnappings start off in offices, buildings play a large part in assault training. These men can been seen getting into position ready to assault on command. The second man is carrying a shotgun which will fire the Hatton round. The Hatton round is a special 12-bore cartridge case which will remove the hinge and a large section of a door. (P)

When the 'GO' is given, the assault team will make their entry. This picture shows the Hatton round about to be fired while the rest of the team make ready. The man on the end is holding a Hooligan bar. (P)

The Hooligan bar being put through its paces. It was designed in America for the express purpose of removing windows. Two or three blows with the bar will take out most of the window, then the hooks are used to pull out the debris. (P)

Planning an assault takes into consideration every possible method of entry. Here two men are attempting to get in through a skylight. The second man, covering, is using an Arwen (shown in detail inset) to fire gas rounds, although it is capable of firing several other different types of projectile. (P)

Repelling down a rope and smashing through a window may look a bit dramatic, but sometimes it is the only solution. The rope feeds from a sack attached to the soldier's leg harness. This avoids any entanglement. (P)

Once an entry has been effected, the first things to go in are the stun grenades and, if deemed necessary, the gas rounds. This is a wonderful shot taken during training just as the assault team is about to enter. (P)

Targets are acquired by searching through the gas or smoke created by the grenades. The laser then 'pings' the target, and the terrorist is history. (P)

The teams have to work through the light and sound of the stun grenades, clearing rooms and stairwells as they go. In this instance, gas has been used. (P)

A dramatic shot of two assault men firing, set against a backdrop of fire caused by a stun grenade. This is a minor fault with the stun grenade, but one the SAS are able to put up with considering the spectacular effect and advantages of the grenade. (P)

During any SAS terrorist operation, marksmen from the police D11 section are always in evidence. They normally supply the outer cordon surrounding the area of operations, and assist with the handling of the situation until the SAS are on the scene. This man is using a Tikka Finlander .223 sniper rifle. The man behind him is spotting. (P)

This picture highlights the diversity and manoeuvrability of the SAS. Using a Chinook helicopter, they descend and assault the hijacked bus. The men can descend, complete with ladders and equipment, in only seconds. The elements of speed and surprise play a major part in any such operation. (1989) (P)

Trains can be attacked using the same technique. You will note by the smashed window that no expense is spared during training. British Rail and the Unions were both consulted about the first-ever practice train assault. They gave their full cooperation; their only stipulation was that the rolling stock be moveable at the end of the day. (1985) (P)

SAS divers can get aboard almost any vessel, even while at sea. Specialised equipment allows them to climb up from the sea and board the vessel in silence. These pictures show the men getting from the water, up the flexi ladders, and on to the deck. (1990) (P)

Hijackings are still an important weapon in the terrorist arsenal, but new techniques are constantly under development to keep the SAS ahead of the game. Assault teams can board any major airliner in seconds, using the same vehicle platforms that are used for a house assault. Note the double ladders. This allows one man to open the door while the next man can immediately enter the aircraft. (P)

While his partners are effecting an entry, the back-up is always ready, should any terrorists show themselves. (P)

An assault team member with his respirator slipped over his elbow. This ensures it is instantly available. (P)

Opposite: Once inside the aircraft little will stop the SAS man from quickly locating the terrorists and neutralising them. Protected by the best armour money can buy and highly trained in state-of-the-art weaponry, the SAS anti-terrorist soldier is a mean beast. (P)

In addition to his skill as a marksman, the SAS sniper must be an expert in camouflage and concealment. This SAS anti-terrorist team sniper is fully dressed in a 'Gilly' suit. The picture was taken around 1976 and shows the sniper using a Tikka Finlander rifle fitted with night sight. He is also wearing an S6 respirator. (P)

Opposite top: A close-up shot of an SAS sniper using a Tikka Finlander. Although respirators are not always necessary for the anti-terrorist snipers, they still practise just in case. (P)

Opposite bottom: SAS sniper training is to Olympic standards. The men shown here are shooting from a range of 300m at head-sized moving targets. Snipers are trained to shoot simultaneously, on command, and are expected to hit all the targets. (1978) (P)

Above: For shorter-range targets, the anti-terrorist team have taken to using the Heckler & Koch G3 sniper rifle. The sniper, seen here taking a rest, is dressed for the urban role.

Above right: This sniper is fully kitted out in his 'Gilly' suit and is carrying an Accuracy International PM. This is a 7.62mm bolt action sniper rifle produced in Britain and adopted by the army as L96 A1. It is fitted with a bipod, and carries a ten-round magazine. The sight is normally a Schmidt and Bender. Accuracy International also produce a suppressed (silenced) version. (Photo Press)

Opposite top: This picture was taken in the early days of sniper training. The soldier here is using an old L42. (P)

Opposite bottom: SAS snipers are also expected to operate in the urban environment. This sniper in the doorway of a building will not be further than 50 metres from his target. (P)

CHAPTER EIGHT

COUNTER REVOLUTIONARY WARFARE

The anti-terrorist team grew from the need to establish a Counter Revolutionary Warfare capability within the SAS. The Counter Revolutionary Wing (CRW) from which the anti-terrorist team would emerge, came into being in the early 70s literally overnight. A squad was sent directly to the Rover factory, commandeering the next four white Range Rovers from the production line (they now use black ones). It appears that the Prime Minister himself had intervened to authorise the immediate procurement of the vehicles and whatever other specialist equipment the new unit required. The team quickly grew into a full Squadron commitment, with the anti-terrorist team well to the fore.

While the anti-terrorist team deals mainly with domestic incidents within the UK, the Counter Revolutionary Wing (CRW) is active all over the world, collating information about terrorist and militant groups and working with the intelligence agencies of our own as well as other governments in a bid to combat the international terrorist problem. Knowledge is everything in the fight against terrorism and it is CRW which provides the anti-terrorist team with information about their enemy and the best tactics to use to get the job done.

CRW is, therefore, heavily involved in the development of CQB (Close Quarter Battle) skills. As well as covering the assault techniques used by the anti-terrorist team, CRW is involved in close protection work for VIPs including the royal family, members of parliament and visiting foreign dignitaries. All SAS soldiers are trained in CRW procedures and many, on leaving the regiment, find work as bodyguards for politicians and heads in countries throughout the world.

A stunning picture taken during the re-enactment of the Iranian Embassy siege. The men are actually on the roof of the building next door to the embassy. (Mirror)

This picture shows the SAS during a bodyguard course. They are debussing from their vehicle, firing as they go. The prime directive in any assault by the enemy is to protect the VIP. In many cases this means shielding him with your own body. (P)

In the fight against terrorism, especially when protecting VIPs, a special range of weapons has been developed. The main picture shows the Heckler & Koch MP5K being fitted into a special briefcase. The weapon is loaded and made ready to fire with the safety catch off. Once the case is closed, safety and firing is controlled by a trigger and safety catch built into the handle. The bottom picture shows the weapons being fired on full automatic.

These pictures show a typical bodyguard situation. The principle (VIP) is just leaving his hotel and comes under fire from an assassin. The reaction of his bodyguards is instant. Weapons are out and the principle is already being shielded and pushed to safety. Seconds later, as the assassin is dropped, the principle is gone and the bodyguards back away. The pictures were taken during the making of a video about SAS techniques. The men are all ex-SAS hired for the part.

This close-up of the Heckler & Koch MP5K shows the special covert harness used to conceal the weapon under the bodyguard's jacket. The weapon is attached to a swivel which allows it to swing into immediate action.

Protection of the royal family is another role undertaken by the SAS. It is wise to let any VIPs know what could be in store for them one day, should they ever have to be rescued. Understanding what might be required of them in a live situation will help the VIPs to react appropriately when the time comes. Here we see Princess Anne in a rescue scenario.

These rare pictures show both Prince Charles and Princess Diana taking part in hostage training. The poor quality of the inset photograph is due to the darkness and smoke inside the 'Killing House'. While Prince Charles seems to be enjoying the demonstration, Princess Diana is protecting herself against the ordeal. All the targets around the royal couple have have been hit with several rounds. Both the royals seem much more at ease posing with some of the anti-terrorist team members after the exercise. (P)

Hostage rescue is designed to cover all situations. These hostages are about to be released, but not before they have been handcuffed and vetted. The SAS treat everyone as a suspected terrorist until all the survivors have been positively identified. (P)

The outdoor range above was constructed literally overnight in the desert in Saudi Arabia where the SAS were training a Saudi anti-terrorist team. The SAS instructors can be seen preparing the students for range practice. (P)

All shooting skills require lots of range work. Learning to identify the terrorist from the hostage in a split second forms part of this training. (P)

The SAS instruct many other nations in anti-terrorist and bodyguard techniques. This action against a hijacked bus is again in Saudi Arabia. The picture on the right shows the author, who had been promoted for the duration of the assignment to captain, with officers of the Saudi team. (P)

For security reasons, it is not possible to relate many of the operations in which the CRW has been involved abroad, but one which can be mentioned happened in The Gambia on 30 July 1981. While the Gambian President was in Britain attending the wedding of Prince Charles and Lady Diana Spencer, rebels seized the capital, Banjul. Prime Minister Margaret Thatcher ordered the SAS to send a small team to Gambia to check out the situation. The two-man SAS team not only rescued the President's wife and children, but they then led troops from neighbouring Senegal against the rebels. After four days the coup had collapsed and the two SAS men slipped back into Britain. This picture is of Princess Anne with President Jawara. (Frank Spooner)

This picture was taken just minutes after the Italian Prime Minister Aldo Moro was kidnapped on 16 March 1978. All his bodyguards were killed and he was taken hostage by Red Brigade terrorists. The CRW had a team in Italy helping to try to track down the kidnappers but, despite the massive effort to locate the Prime Minister, he was eventually found murdered on 9 May.

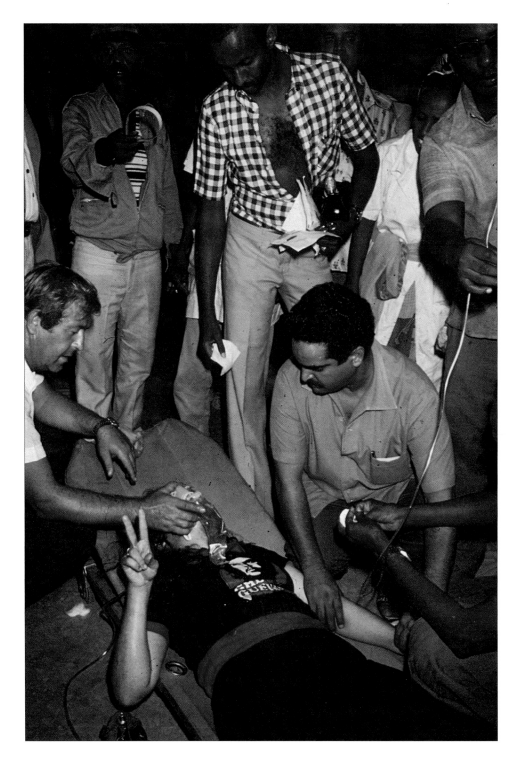

On 13 October 1977, Mogadishu was the scene of a dramatic aircraft assault by the German GSG9 and SAS. The British Prime Minister, Harold Wilson, had directed the SAS to assist the German anti-terrorist team after an appeal from the German Chancellor. While assaulting the Lufthansa 737, three of the four Palestinian terrorists were killed, but one, Souhaila Sayeh, survived. This picture was taken just a few moments after the hostages had all been successfully released. As Souhaila was led away on a stretcher, she gave the 'Victory V' sign.

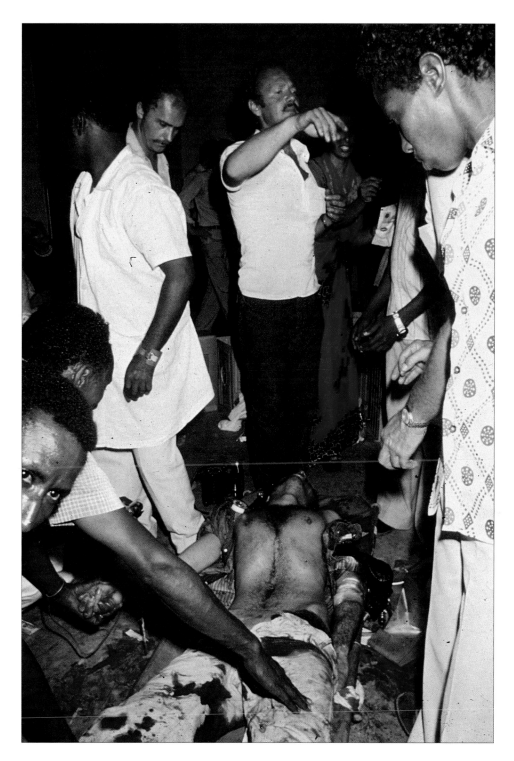

The picture is of the dead terrorist leader Mahmud (real name Zohair Akache). He had knelt the German pilot Jurgen Schumann in the aisle of the aircraft and shot him through the head. He believed that Schumann had been passing information about the hijackers to the security forces. Mahmud was an out-and-out killer. Just a few months prior to the hijack he had been in London where he had assassinated the ex-premier of North Yemen, his wife, and a Yemeni diplomat outside the Bayswater Hotel.

At 11.25am on the morning of Wednesday 30 April 1980, along the tree-lined avenue of Princes Gate, in London's Kensington district, six armed gunmen took over No. 16 - the Iranian Embassy. Armed D11 marksmen soon surrounded the building and the siege negotiating plans were put into operation. The anti-terrorist team in Hereford were at this time practising in the 'Killing House', but things were soon to change. By 11.47 the Metropolitan Police were talking to the Commanding Officer in Hereford and the CRW were assessing the situation. Six days later, when negotiations collapsed after the murder of the embassy press attache, the SAS were ordered in. This picture is of the assault team entering the front of the embassy just seconds after the explosive frame charge had removed the complete window.

This picture was taken by one of the D11 police snipers. The embassy is on fire but the assault team presses on with its task. Note the SAS men lined up by the back wall. These men received the hostages as they came out of the building and took them to the small grass area just visible in the bottom left corner. (P)

As the assault teams went in the front, SAS men abseiled down the rear of the building and smashed their way in through the back. The abseil lines had been carefully set up in advance (see left) but one of the soldiers still had the bad luck to become entangled - carrying the abseil line in a leg harness now helps to prevent this - and received severe burns while suspended above a blazing window. When he was cut free, he fell to the balcony, picked himself up and entered the building, promptly shooting one of the terrorists dead. (P)

Opposite: The whole assault was dramatic to say the least. With the embassy on fire, and the sound of automatic gunfire coming from every direction, the SAS were being hailed as heroes. When it was over, five of the six terrorists were dead, and only one of the twenty hostages was lost, killed by the terrorists. The SAS then disappeared back to Hereford. This picture was taken inside the embassy in the aftermath of the battle.

CHAPTER NINE

THE FALKLANDS

When the Argentines invaded the Falkland Islands on 2 April 1982, they thought they were in an unassailable position. They reckoned without the resolve of a strong British Government. Despite the great distances involved and the small number of British subjects who inhabited these isolated South Atlantic islands, Prime Minister Thatcher vowed that the people of the Falklands would not be abandoned and decided to retake the islands by force.

Within a couple of weeks, plans were well advanced for the taking of South Georgia, a small group of islands some 800 miles from the Falklands, also now in the hands of the Argentines. Initially, the SAS role was one of surveillance and intelligence gathering, supplying vital information from which the commanders, most of whom where still at sea in the largest armada to set sail since World War II, could develop their invasion plans.

By the beginning of May, SAS and SBS reconnaissance patrols were checking out sites for a large-scale landing. Living in terrible conditions, they were constantly on the move, always hiding from the Argentines. The hides were mainly small caves or clusters of rock, damp and wet, constantly battered by the island weather. To avoid detection by the Argentines, the patrols were forced to hike many miles away from their OPs each night in order to signal back to base without their transmissions giving away their positions.

Although they scored many successes during the Falklands campaign, the conflict took a heavy toll on the regiment with eighteen men lost in one incident when a Sea King helicopter crashed into the sea while transferring them from one ship to another. The contribution made by the SAS in the retaking of the islands cannot be underestimated.

The SAS raid on Pebble Island on the night of 14/15 May was a classic operation involving Boat Troop and Mountain Troop of D Squadron. A reconnaissance patrol had landed by canoe three nights earlier. They were joined by 45 men who were inserted by helicopter. They attacked and destroyed six Pucara aircraft (including the one in this photo), four Turbo-Mentors and a Shorts Skyvan, setting fire to vast amounts of ammunition and stores in the process. The raiding party withdrew in good order with only one slight casualty. While they were waiting for the helicopter pick-up, a further Pucara was shot down with a 'stinger' missile.

One of the first tasks undertaken by the SAS during the Falklands
campaign was to set up observation posts on the island of South Georgia.
The first attempt, on 22 April, finished as a disaster. The party was
dropped by helicopter on to the Fortuna Glacier and quickly realised that
to stay there meant certain death: The weather was so bad that they
would all have died of exposure within hours and an immediate recall was
requested. The extraction cost two Wessex helicopters, both of which
crashed in the appalling weather. A piece of brilliant flying on the part of
a third pilot, in a severely overladen chopper and in blind flying
conditions, led to the rescue of every single man. Undeterred, the SAS
eventually landed on the island by boat. They observed the Argentine
garrison at Grytviken, comprising of about 100 marines and the crew of
the submarine Santa Fe, which was in the harbour delivering supplies. A
British force made up of SBS, SAS and Royal Marines attacked the base
after being landed by helicopter with fire support from the Royal Navy.
The garrison surrendered. It was the first victory of the Falklands War.

Elements of the SAS were inserted into the Falklands three weeks in advance of the main task force to carry out reconnaissance and identify suitable areas for large-scale landings. The SAS lived like hermits in caves or sheltering in rocky outcrops. The cold was unbearable and death from hypothermia was a very real danger. The soldier on the left of this picture is an SAS trooper being extracted as British forces arrive. He has spent a long lonely stint out in the open.

After the main force had landed at San Carlos, the next major objective was Goose Green. As 2 Parachute Regiment fought a brilliant battle to take Goose Green, 3 Para and the Royal Marines moved on the northern end of East Falklands. Between these two forces were the SAS on Mount Kent. They held the position to stop the Argentines outflanking either of the two main battle groups. Both of these pictures were taken during the battle for Goose Green. The school can be seen burning in the background of the shot on the right while the paratrooper above, who went on to join the SAS, is keeping his head down as the bullets fly. (P)

This picture was taken as the Argentines raised their flag on the Falklands.
It was found on the body of a dead Argentine soldier shot by the SAS
close to Mount Kent.

The sinking of HMS *Sheffield* by an Argentine Exocet missile prompted Margaret Thatcher to order one of the most daring raids of the Falklands War. If the raid was successful, it would remove the Exocet threat for good. The raid was to be a full Squadron attack on the airfield of Rio Gallegos on the southern tip of the Argentine mainland. Intelligence reports indicated that this was where the remaining stocks of Exocet would be found. The SAS raiders were to fly the 5000 miles from the British base on Ascension Island in Hercules C130 aircraft, land on the Argentine airfield and destroy the Exocets and as many enemy aircraft as possible. Having created utter mayhem, the SAS were then to run for the border of neutral Chile some 50 miles away.

Thirty-six hours prior to the arrival of the main raiding party, a Royal Navy Sea King helicopter had flown in with an SAS advance party in order to recce the airfield. Due to bad weather, the three-man crew of the Sea King landed the reconnaissance unit on the beach at Punta Arenas, 30 miles from the target. An SAS explosives expert fitted a bomb to the helicopter and destroyed it. The crew were told to make their way to the British Embassy in Chile, telling the story that they had got lost in the bad weather and crashed on the shore. The SAS disappeared. The whole mission was ultimately aborted.

In such a small unit as the SAS, the loss of a single soldier takes its toll. When eighteen are taken in one go, it is devastating. Choppers ferried men and supplies from one ship to another in what was called 'cross-decking' (seen above). A Sea King with a crew of four and 26 passengers, mostly SAS, plunged into the sea from a height of 300ft after a bird strike on its engine. Miraculously, nine men survived.

Left: While Hereford Cathedral opened its doors for people to mourn the loss of so many men whose lives were inevitably interwoven with the local community, a second disaster struck the town. HMS *Antelope*, adopted by a local Hereford pub and seen by many as a 'Hereford' ship, was hit and sunk by an Argentine bomb.

No story of the SAS in the Falklands can conclude without mentioning Captain John Hamilton. He was involved in almost every SAS action of the campaign. As mountain troop officer, he led his men on to the Fortuna Glacier in the bid to take South Georgia. He also took part in the successful raid against the Argentine airfield on Pebble Island. Sadly, he was killed on 10 June when his patrol was spotted during a close-target reconnaissance. During the fire-fight, although wounded, he held the Argentines at bay while the rest of his men made their escape. He was awarded the Military Cross. Unfortunately, no photographs are available of Captain Hamilton.

CHAPTER TEN

THE GULF WAR

On 2 August 1990, Iraqi dictator Saddam Hussein ordered his army into neighbouring Kuwait. The small sheikdom of Kuwait was largely unprepared to defend itself against such an act of aggression and could not, in any case, hope to withstand the might of Saddam's military machine. Swiftly overrun, Kuwait appealed to the rest of the world for help and a coalition of Western states, with the backing of the United Nations and led by the United States, began building an army which would send Saddam packing.

Having captured Kuwait, Saddam was now threatening the borders of Saudi Arabia and it was here that almost half a million men and women of the coalition sweated it out under the scorching desert sun, biding their time until the order came to move against the Iraqis. For the air force and the navy, the war began on 17 January 1991 when Iraqi targets first started to come under attack from wave after wave of aircraft and Tomahawk cruise missile strikes. Sitting on the sidelines amid this frenetic activity, were the SAS.

At first their role in this conflict was unclear. It was proposed that they might try to rescue the hostages who had been seized and used by Saddam Hussein as human shields, being held prisoner in installations likely to be attacked by coalition aircraft or missiles. This, however, was thought to be a near-impossible task and,

ultimately, most of the hostages were released anyway. Then it was decided that they would infiltrate deep into Iraqi territory and carry out search and destroy missions, disrupting communications and destroying targets which were proving problematic for the air force. One of their main priorities was to find and destroy the Scud missiles Saddam was launching against Israel. Saddam's intention was to draw the Israelis into the war, thus wrecking the coalition's support from the Arab nations.

The SAS strength in the Gulf was split into groups. Some would be inserted by helicopter to monitor the main supply routes, while others formed themselves into fighting columns. These columns consisted of 110 Land Rovers and Light Strike Vehicles (LSVs), with motorbikes being used as outriders. The fire-power carried was enough to take on and destroy just about anything they could find. The idea was to create so much mayhem that the Iraqis would have to deploy large forces in order to neutralise the raiders.

For the SAS it was a hard war. The desert terrain of Iraq was not as one normally imagines a desert. It was a harsh cruel place, the enemy were everywhere, and when they were not fighting the Iraqis, they were fighting the bitter cold. Most of the photographs shown in this chapter were taken deep behind the enemy lines, in some cases just a few miles from Baghdad.

As the SAS fighting columns penetrated ever deeper into Iraq, it was inevitable that they should make contact with the enemy. While one column lay camouflaged during the day, the sentry signalled that an enemy vehicle was approaching. Mistaking the SAS for Iraqi forces, the Russian-built Gaz 69 drove straight into the SAS hide. In a short but vicious fire-fight three of the four Iraqis were killed. The survivor, a Major carrying lots of maps and other useful information, was sent back to Saudi by helicopter for interrogation. The Gaz 69, together with the bodies, was destroyed by placing two bar mines under it. Although this picture is not the vehicle in question, it does show the aftermath of a similar encounter.

Last-minute training and preparations for the Gulf War took place in the Trucial States, which is where this Squadron photo was taken. Land Rovers were the main vehicles used throughout the conflict and they carried extensive and varied firepower including the Browning .5 heavy machine gun, GPMGs, 40mm grenade launchers and Milan anti-tank missiles. Thermal imaging sights were fitted to some Land Rovers, giving the operator the advantage of being able to see up to 8km even in total darkness. In the picture you can also see two LSV 'dune buggies'. These lightweight vehicles were dispensed with after they suffered reliability problems in the desert. More of a success were the Honda 250 motorbikes which acted as outriders to a fighting column such as this, scouting ahead for signs of danger and potential targets. (P)

Preparing to enter Iraq from Saudi Arabia. When they were finally given the go-ahead on 20 January, 1991, they simply drove through the Iraqi defence lines. Note the Union Jack spread out on the ground. This was used to indicate to allied aircraft that they were friendly forces. (P)

The fighting column on the move. Note the bike which was
used as an outrider. (P)

To avoid detection, camouflage and concealment were of vital
importance. From a distance the whole column would blend in
with the surrounding terrain. (P)

Beneath the camouflage nets, life went on. By day the SAS would cook, do sentry duty and sleep. By night they would hunt. (P)

This picture was taken after the previously mentioned incident with the Iraqi Gaz 69. The enemy vehicle can be seen underneath the camouflage net. The bodies of the three dead Iraqi soldiers were still in the vehicle at this stage. (P)

As with British fighting men throughout this century, hot tea was always welcome. It kept them warm and helped to keep them alert during the long daylight hours. (P)

Despite the padded clothing, sentry duty lasted no more than two hours per man, then it was back into the sleeping bag. The sentries have an M16 with 203 grenade launcher, a Minimus and a Milan anti-tank missile. (P)

Both pictures demonstrate the vast amount of fire-power carried by the column. Beside one of the sleeping men is an Accuracy International PM sniper rifle. (P)

Even during a routine stop, it was always advisable to post a look-out
sentry. In this picture he can be seen sitting on the ridge. (P)

The 110 Land Rovers carried the fire-power, armed with Browning .5 heavy machine guns, GPMGs, American Mark 19, 40mm grenade launchers and Milan anti-tank missiles. Some were fitted with thermal imaging sights, which meant that they could be see up to 8km away, even in total darkness. (P)

Keeping warm was a major priority, and much of the soldiers' free time was spent in the 'Green Maggot' (sleeping bag). These men show the Arab overcoats that were purchased locally and issued after the first re-supply. The 'shimag' tops off the native look. (P)

The 'shimag' headdress was not just for show. Just as in the desert campaigns of World War II, the soldiers in the Gulf found that the native gear was best for keeping out the dust and keeping off the sun. (P)

In the flat, open countryside of Iraq, the column was normally protected by motorbike out-riders. They would travel in front and to the flanks, constantly searching for the enemy, either as a source of danger or a potential target. (P)

The machine gun and sights seen in this picture would normally be hidden by a protective cover when not in use to keep out the dust of the desert which was a major cause of weapons' malfunctions. (P)

An SAS Corporal shot dead in the Gulf War. The motorcycle outriders of his fighting column spotted two Iraqi trucks laden with missiles heading straight towards them. The column did not have time to set up a proper ambush but pulled off the road to prepare for a fight. They were spotted as the two trucks rolled past and the Iraqis sped off. The motorbike riders gave chase. As one trooper described it, 'It was a little like the Indians chasing the train in the Wild West.' The bikes forced the trucks to stop but as the main force of Land Rovers engaged the enemy, two of the men on bikes were caught in the cross-fire. One was killed, and the other seriously wounded.

This LSV has broken down and is being fixed with parts carried by the Unimog support vehicle. (P)

Serious battle damage was repaired whenever possible beneath the camouflage nets while the troops rested up during the daytime. During a vehicle re-supply a complete field workshop was set up inside Iraq where all the SAS vehicles were serviced. (P)

Re-supplying the columns was done by Chinook helicopter, and three tonne trucks. (P)

The choppers or trucks never hung around long. Once the re-supply was dropped off, it was up to the column to sort out the mess. This re-supply by truck shows the amount of supplies needed to keep a fighting column on the move. These photographs were taken deep behind Iraqi lines. (P)

All enemy movement was logged and reported. Here the signaller is
encoding a message back to base in Saudi Arabia. Once the Scud war
started they were constantly on the look-out for the launchers. One of the
major reasons the Israelis never entered the war was the fact that they
were informed that the SAS were already doing the job. (P)

Opposite: The chest harness worn here contains mainly ammunition. The
main weapon on the Land Rover is a .50 cal machine gun. The men would
be fully dressed while they were moving or while on sentry duty. (P)

A fighting column could spread out over quite some distance while travelling through the desert and regular stops were made to keep all the vehicles together. (P)

Final preparation before the attack on a microwave communications station known as Victor two. This attack was carried out by a whole fighting column, and was the largest single attack carried out by the SAS during the Gulf War. While some are planning the attack others are getting what rest they can. (P)

Deep behind the Iraqi lines, it is essential to identify yourself as friendly
forces, hence the Union Jack was always kept handy. (P)

The value of having the SAS operating behind the enemy lines was not known until after the war was over. Here members of the SAS are being congratulated by General Norman Schwarzkopf. (P)

CHAPTER ELEVEN

SPECIALS AND SURPRISES

Over the years the SAS has participated in many actions around the world and, just sometimes, you can snap a picture that to the normal civilian is quite bizarre. I have included in this short chapter pictures which I feel should be shown. Some are directly related to the SAS, and some touch the sidelines. They are not in any order, but there is an explanation as to why each picture is special.

Many people perceive members of the SAS to be little more than highly trained killers and, as a tax payer, that is basically what you pay for. But I hope that these few photographs will open your eyes to a different side of the regiment. Some of the pictures are sad, some are funny, and all of them are unique.

This picture of a solid gold winged dagger hails from the Gulf War. Most of the SAS soldiers were issued with gold sovereigns to aid their escape, should it be necessary. Once the war was over, of course, not all of the sovereigns were returned. Some were used by soldiers in trouble to buy vehicles or help, while others were lost along with other (more valuable) pieces of kit. In the heat of battle, equipment often has to be ditched. During my research for this book, I learned of the existence of this Golden Winged Dagger. It was hand crafted by a master jeweller in the Middle East from thirteen gold sovereigns issued to an SAS soldier. The jeweller took two coins in payment and the remaining five coins carried by the soldier are pictured with the dagger. The soldier in question genuinely believed the coins had been lost with part of his kit. When they later turned up, the Golden Winged Dagger seemed like a good idea.

During the late 60s there was little for the regiment to do. For many,
training filled the gap, while others went in search of new adventures.
This picture is of a power boat, manned by the SAS during a race.

These pictures were taken during the first army course on paragliding. One of the armoured divisions stationed in Germany lent a hut to house the course. NAAFI purchased the parachutes, and the author organised the whole event. Paragliding is now a recognised adventure activity in the British Army. The main picture is of the author flying.

As a footnote to the 1977 Mogadishu hijack, the surviving female terrorist, Souhaila Andraws (her married name), finally finished up in Norway. In order to hear her side of the story, I went to visit her. What she told me led me to interview several of the hostages and the wife of the murdered pilot, Captain Schumann. Eventually, I persuaded Monica Schumann to meet Souhaila Andraws in the hope that some peaceful understanding would emerge. In December 1995, Souhaila Andraws was flown to Germany, where she is currently on trial for her part in the hijack. This picture shows her in a Norwegian hotel before her extradition. *From left to right:* Monica Schumann, myself, Heidi Bache-Wug (Souhaila's lawyer) and Souhaila Andraws.

Mrs Thatcher thanking boys in Northern Ireland.

A funny picture of two SAS officers with some captured weapons. Why funny? Well, you will note the officer on the right has a broken finger. When a fixed wing aircraft was sent in to evacuate this casualty, the aircraft damaged its landing gear. A helicopter was sent to sky-hook the damaged aircraft out. As this was happening the under-slung aircraft became unstable and a jet fighter was dispatched to check the undercarriage of the helicopter. The oscillations of the aircraft were ripping the hell out of the helicopter bottom, so they decided to drop the aircraft and write if off. As the jet returned to the airfield, it suffered a bird strike directly into the jet engine and the pilot was forced to eject. In total, the bill ran into millions. As far as I can recollect, the officer was eventually driven to hospital in a Land Rover.

At times throughout this book I have referred to the similarities between the SAS past and present. These two pictures were taken some 40 years apart. The top one is of David Stirling in the desert and I am led to believe that the bottom one was taken on exercise in Africa, around the 1980s.

CHAPTER TWELVE

ROLL OF HONOUR

This special stained-glass window in St Martin's Church in Hereford was produced in honour of the Special Air Service. It stands as tribute to all those SAS men who have died in the service of their country and now lie in the graveyard of the church. What many people will not be aware of is how small (in numbers) the SAS really is. It is safe to say that, although the regiment continues to be topped up with new recruits passing selection, since 1950 the death toll has risen to more than half the regiment's combat strength. The price of democracy, freedom and liberty does not come cheap.

SAS CASUALTIES 1950 TO 1995

MALAYA

TPR T. A. BROWN	1950
PTE G. A. FISHER	1950
TPR J. A. O'LEARY	1951
SGT O. H. ERNST, *Rhodesian SAS*	1951
CPL J. B. DAVIES, *Rhodesian SAS*	1951
TPR F. G. BOYLAN	1951
WO2 W. F. GARRETT	1951
CPL V. E. VISAGUE, *Rhodesian SAS*	1952
TPR A. FERGUS	1952
MAJ E. C. R. BARKER, BEM	1953
TPR J. A. S. MORGAN	1953
TPR E. DUCKWORTH	1953
LT P. B. S. CARTWRIGHT	1953
TPR B. WATSON	1953
2/LT F. M. DONNELLY-WOOD	1953
LT (QM) F. S. TULK	1953
CPL K. BANCROFT	1953
TPR F. W. WILKINS	1953
CPL P. G. R. EAKIN	1953
LT J. C. FOTHERINGHAN	1953
LT G. J. GOULDING	1954
L CPL C. W. BOND	1954
TPR B. POWELL	1954

TPR A. W. HOWELL	1954
TPR A. R. THOMAS *New Zealand SAS*	1956
TPR W. R. J. MARSELLE	1956
LT A. G. H. DEAN	1957
CPL A. G. BUCHANAN *New Zealand SAS*	1957
TPR R. HINDMARSH	1968

OMAN (JEBEL AKHDAR)

CPL D. SWINDELLS, M. M.	1958
TPR W. CARTER	1959
TPR A. G. BEMBRIDGE	1959

BORNEO

MAJ H. A. I. THOMPSON MC	1963
MAJ R. H. D. NORMAN, MBE, MC	1963
CPL M. P. MURPHY	1963
TPR A. CONDON	1964
SGT B. BEXTON	1964
TPR W. E. WHITE	1964
PTE G. H. HARTLEY	1964

WEST MALAYSIA

L CPL R. GREENWOOD	1967

MALAYSIA

TPR N. P. OLLIS	1969

SOUTH ARABIA

CAPT R. C. EDWARDS	1964
TPR J. N. WARBURTON	1964
TPR J. HOLLINGSWORTH	1964
TPR M. R. LAMBERT	1966
TPR G. F. F. ILES	1967
L CPL A. G. BROWN	1967

ETHIOPIA

CPL I. A. MACLEOD	1968

OMAN (MUSANDAM)

L CPL P. REDDY	1970

OMAN (DHOFAR)

CAPT I. E. JONES	1971
SGT J. S. M. MOORES	1971
TPR C. LOID	1971
L CPL D. R. RAMSDEN	1972
TPR M. J. MARTIN	1972
CPL T. LABALABA, BEM	1972
TPR T. P. A. TOPIN	1972
L CPL A. KENT	1974
CAPT S. GARTHWAITE	1974
TPR C. HENNESSY	1975
L CPL K. SMALL	1975
SGT A. E. GALLAGHER	1975

BRUNEI

SGT E. PICKARD	1973
SGT G. GREEN	1989

FRANCE

MAJ R. M. PIRIE	1972
SGT S. H. JOHNSON	1978
CPL F. M. BENSON	1978
TPR R. P. ARNOTT	1986
TPR S. J. WINDON	1986

NORTHERN IRELAND

S/SGT D. J. NADEN	1978
CAPT H. R. WESTMACOTT, MC	1980
CPL T. PALMER, MM	1983
L CPL A. SLATER, MM	1984

UK

CPL K. NORRY	1962
CPL R. RICHARDSON	1965
TPR P. C. O'TOOLE	1965
TPR J. HOOKER	1965
L CPL J. R. ANDERSON	1967
L CPL A. C. LONNEY	1968
WO1 E. T. NUGENT	1968
CPL R. N. ADIE	1968

TPR C. P. MARTIN	1968
WO2 J. E. DAUBNEY	1974
MAJ M. J. A. KEALY, DSO	1979
SGT R. ABBOTS	1985
SGT A. BAXTER	1985
S/SGT J. DRUMMOND	1986
TPR G. WORRALL	1990
CPL A. FLEMMING, MBE (wounded in Dhofar 1975)	1994

SOUTH ATLANTIC

CAPT G. J. HAMILTON	1982
WO2 L. GALLAGHER, BEM	1982
SGT P. P. CURRASS, QGM	1982
SGT S. A. I. DAVIDSON	1982
SGT J. L. ARTHY	1982
CPL P. BUNKER	1982
CPL E. T. WALPOLE	1982
TRP R. ARMSTRONG	1982
SSM M. ATKINSON	1982
S/SGT P. O'CONNOR	1982
SGT W. J. HUGHES	1982
SGT P. JONES	1982
CPL W. J. BEGLEY	1982
CPL J. NEWTON	1982
CPL S. SYKES	1982
L CPL P. LIGHTFOOT	1982
CPL M. McHUGH	1982
FLT LT G. HAWKINS	1982
CPL D. McCORMACK	1982

BELIZE

L SGT L. COBB	1983
L CPL M. D. RICHARDS	1992

MOUNT EVEREST

CPL A. SWIERZY	1984

BOTSWANA

S/SGT K. J. FARRAGHER	1986

FAR EAST

Cpl P. Hill	1988

IRAQ

SGT V. PHILLIPS	1991
TRP R. CONSIGLIO, MM	1991
TRP S. LANE, MM	1991
TPR . D DENBURY, MM	1991

BOSNIA

CPL F. M. RENNIE	1994

SAS Operational History

1941 - North Africa
14 December Agheila Enemy airfield raid
21 December Agedabai Enemy airfield raid

1942 - North Africa
8 March Barce Enemy airfield raid
Berka Enemy airfield raid
25 March Benina Enemy airfield raid
13 June Benina Enemy airfield raid
13 June Berka Enemy airfield raid
7 July Bagoush Enemy Airfield raid
El Daba Enemy airfield raid
Fuka Enemy airfield raid
12 July Fuka Enemy airfield raid
26 July Sidi Haneish Enemy airfield raid

1943 - Sicily
12 July Operation Chestnut Supporting allied invasion of Sicily

1943 - Italy
3 September Operation Baytown Port of Bagnara captured
7 September Operation Speedwell Raid in north east Italy
2-6 October Operation Begonia Aiding British POWs
27 October Operation Candytuft Attack on railway communications

1944 - Italy
7 January Operation Maple Supporting Anzio landings
30 January Operation Baobab Supporting Anzio landings

1944 - France
6 June Operation Titanic Raiding mission in Normandy
6 June Operation Dingson Raiding mission in Brittany
6-9 June Operation Samwest Raiding mission in Brittany
6-21 June Operation Houndsworth Attacks on railway communications
6 June-3 July Operation Bullbasket Attacks on railway communications
6 June-15 August Operation Gain Attacks on communication, south of Paris
7 June Operation Cooney Attacks on railway communications
23 June-18 July Operation Lost Raiding mission and arming Maquis in Brittany
8 July-11 August Operation Haft Intelligence mission
16 July-7 October Operation Dickens Attacks on railway communications in Nantes
19 July-23 August Operation Defoe Reconnaissance mission in Normandy

23 July-10 September Operation Rupert Attacks on railway communications
25 July Operation Gaff Assassination attempt on Rommel
27 July-1 September Operation Hardy Raiding mission in Dijon
28 July-15 August Operation Chaucer Raiding mission in north west
31 July-15 August Operation Shakespeare Raiding mission in north west
3-15 August Operation Bunyan Raiding mission in north west
3-24 August Operation Dunhill Intelligence mission
5-18 August Operation Derry Harrassing enemy near Brest
10-23 August Operation Haggard Engaging enemy at River Loire
10 August-27 September Operation Samson Raiding mission in the south
11-24 August Operation Marshall General attacks on enemy
12 August-9 October Operation Loyton Intelligence mission
13-24 August Operation Snelgrove Supplying arms to resistance
13 August-19 September Operation Barker Supporting US advance
13 August-24 September Operation Harrod Attacking enemy troop movements
13 August-26 September Operation Kipling Major enemy engagement
15 August-9 September Operation Jockworth Engaging enemy in south east
16 August-13 September Operation Noah Intelligence mission
19 August-11 September Operation Newton Harrassing enemy
19 August-19 September Operation Wallace Major enemy engagement
26 August-3 September Operation Wolsey Intelligence mission
28 August-1 September Operation Benson Intelligence mission
29 August-14 September Operation Spenser Harrassing the enemy
15 September-3 October Attacks on railway communications

1944 - Belgium
2 September-15 September Operation Brutus Intelligence mission
6-11 September Operation Caliban Attacks on enemy communications

1944-45 - Holland
16 September-14 March Operation Fabian Intelligence mission
27 September-17 March Operation Gobbo Intelligence mission

1944-1945 - FRANCE

24 December-25 January Operation Franklin Supporting US advance in Ardennes

27 December-15 January Operation Regent Engaging enemy in Ardennes

1944-45 - ITALY

27 December-14 February Operation Galia Intelligence mission

4 March-24 April Operation Tombola Engaging enemy

1945 - HOLLAND

3-18 April Operation Keystone Engaging enemy

1945 - GERMANY

March-May Operation Archway Suporting British advance

3 April-8 May Operation Larkswood Engaging enemy

6 April-6 May Operation Howard Engaging enemy

1945 - NORWAY

May Operation Apostle Disarming German forces

British SAS regiments disbanded October 1945

1950-1960 - MALAYA

Malayan Scouts (SAS) formed Operations against communist-backed guerillas

1951

Formation of 22 SAS

1958-1959 - OMAN

November-January Jebel Akhdar Operations against communist-backed rebels

1963-1966 - BORNEO

Operations against rebels and Indonesian forces

1964-1967 - ADEN

Operations against terrorist rebels prior to British withdrawl

1969 ONWARDS - NORTHERN IRELAND

Operations begin against terrorists in the province

1970-1976 - OMAN

Operations against communist-backed rebels

1972 - OMAN

19 July - Mirbat - SAS team leads local force in successful defence against vastly superior rebel force

1980 - UK

5 May Iranian Embassy Siege, London

1981 - THE GAMBIA

30 July-6 August SAS team puts down coup against President Jawara

1982 - SOUTH ATLANTIC

Intelligence and raiding operations during the Falklands campaign

1988 - GIBRALTAR

6 March SAS team kills three terrorists during IRA bomb mission

1989 ONWARDS - CENTRAL AMERICA

Covert and international co-operative operations in the war against drugs

1991 - IRAQ

Intelligence, raiding and seek-and-destroy missions during the Gulf War